Rescuing Railway Children

Rescuing Railway Children
Reuniting Families from India's Railway Platforms

Malcolm Harper
Lalitha Iyer
with an invited contribution
from Kate Bulman

SAGE www.sagepublications.com
Los Angeles • London • New Delhi • Singapore • Washington DC

First published in 2013 by

 SAGE Publications India Pvt Ltd
B1/I-1 Mohan Cooperative Industrial Area
Mathura Road, New Delhi 110 044, India
www.sagepub.in

SAGE Publications Inc
2455 Teller Road
Thousand Oaks, California 91320, USA

SAGE Publications Ltd
1 Oliver's Yard, 55 City Road
London EC1Y 1SP, United Kingdom

SAGE Publications Asia-Pacific Pte Ltd
33 Pekin Street
#02-01 Far East Square
Singapore 048763

Published by Vivek Mehra for SAGE Publications India Pvt Ltd, Phototypeset in 10.5/12.5 Sabon by RECTO Graphics, Delhi and printed at Saurabh Printers Pvt Ltd, New Delhi.

Library of Congress Cataloging-in-Publication Data Available

ISBN: 978-81-321-1161-0 (HB)

The SAGE Team: Neelakshi Chakraborty, Shreya Lall, Anju Saxena and Rajinder Kaur.

To children striving to make the best of tough situations.

Thank you for choosing a SAGE product! If you have any comment, observation or feedback, I would like to personally hear from you. Please write to me at <u>contactceo@sagepub.in</u>

—Vivek Mehra, Managing Director and CEO,
SAGE Publications India Pvt Ltd, New Delhi

Bulk Sales

SAGE India offers special discounts for purchase of books in bulk. We also make available special imprints and excerpts from our books on demand.

For orders and enquiries, write to us at

Marketing Department
SAGE Publications India Pvt Ltd
B1/I-1, Mohan Cooperative Industrial Area
Mathura Road, Post Bag 7
New Delhi 110044, India
E-mail us at <u>marketing@sagepub.in</u>

Get to know more about SAGE, be invited to SAGE events, get on our mailing list. Write today to <u>marketing@sagepub.in</u>

This book is also available as an e-book.

————ꠁꠒ————

Contents

List of Tables

List of Figures

List of Boxes

Abbreviations

APSA	Association for Promoting Social Action, Bangalore
CWC	Child Welfare Committee
DCPS	District Child Protection Services
GRP	Government Railway Police
ICPS	Integrated Child Protection Scheme
IPSC	Integrated Programme for Street Children
JJ Act	Juvenile Justice (Care and Protection) Act
JJB	Juvenile Justice Board
MWCD	Ministry of Women and Child Development
NCPCR	The National Commission for Protection of Child Rights
NGO	Non-Governmental Organisation
RPF	Railway Protection Force
SBT	Salam Balak Trust
SCPS	State Child Protection Services
SJPU	Special Juvenile Police Unit

Foreword

Many NGOs have pioneered the work to help children seen on the railway platforms, examples being SAATHI Mumbai, BOSCO Bangalore, SBT New Delhi and SNDT Pune. Children on platforms are separated from families, and surviving alone or in groups on platforms. Obviously these children are very vulnerable and there is a need to offer quick help to all of them. The number of children arriving on the platforms is very large and the situation is of concern. Much is written about the lives of the children on the platforms and streets and the dangers they are exposed to. A lot of these writings are anecdotal, and case based. The number of cases covered is still very small compared to the size of the problem.

Our team at Sathi (initially at Raichur, then at Bangalore and now spread to locations in nine states) started helping these children by reuniting them back with their families. Reuniting is done only where the families are found to have the capability to care for the child, and a large number families are indeed capable. Sathi has taken this work forward, covering many locations and helped a large number of children. There was an anxiety, whether these children, reunited with home, will continue to stay with families. In a majority of the situations, children are retained back in families, to the joy of all. Placing children back in their home seems to be a feasible, effective solution to this grim problem. Perhaps this may work for children on the street too.

Placing children back with their families is a complex task. Counselling children, identifying and resolving the issues on account of which the child left home, and continuing support to the child back home has to be done. These processes should meet all requirements of the child's safety and the norms expected as per child protection systems. Sathi cannot claim to be perfect in all these tasks. There were no precedents for many of these tasks when we started. There are many recurring questions. When do we reunite the child back home? What is 'good quality' rehabilitation of the child back home? What explains the high retention rates? Can retention be an indicator of good rehabilitation? There are no ready answers, much less, demonstrations of significant scale across location, or reliable comparison of alternate approaches of rehabilitation of platform children.

The issue of children going missing is of national concern. Our experience has shown that this issue can be addressed. In our view if railway platforms in some 70 towns are covered and all children arriving there are contacted, it would solve a third of the problem at least. The portal for data on 'missing children' and 'found children' captured and fed in an e-system will quicken the process of tracing a missing child.

We are keen to share our experiences of helping 35,000 children in two decades to generate an informed debate. We have experienced great joy in reuniting children with parents and this is worth sharing too. We therefore requested Dr Lalitha Iyer and Prof Malcolm Harper to write on these issues, using our experiences at Sathi and also touching on the experience of other NGOs. Both are acknowledged writers on social issues. Ms Mahalakshmi Sundarraman has helped enthusiastically with the editing in bringing all the material together. Our experience demonstrates what can be done and the book presents this hope. We wish that the government including central and state administration, NGO leaders, child protection systems and campaigners and donors will understand and commit on covering all platforms and clearly budget for family reintegration as a priority.

In addition to sharing what we do, the book also covers the actual functioning of government institutions and systems meant for children in 'need and protection'. Many of these institutions are doing well, and are becoming more robust. But still they need to be more proactive and work as transit institutions rather than being reactive and stagnant systems. This book, we hope, will offer ideas on how to make these systems work better.

It is also our hope that this book generates debate on why children run away from families, and are on the street, and on the norms for their rehabilitation back with families or in other institutions. We hope that the issues along with the solutions practised are brought in the public domain, so that all those concerned about the issues of children ponder to evolve better practices. This, we are sure, will generate more focus and resources for helping the large numbers of such children. We also hope that this book gives ideas as to how to track missing children on a significant scale.

We invite all readers to get in touch with us if they wish to engage more directly with the issues we are grappling.

Bangalore
4 August 2013

Pramod Kulkarni
Secretary at Sathi

Note to the Reader

Many children who have run away from their homes arrive on the major railway platforms in India every day. There are also children who lose their way or get accidentally separated from the adults they are with. This book is about the challenges faced by these children who see no easy way to get back home.

The first chapter presents an overview of the situation in India bringing together the estimates of the number of such children, the challenges they face on the platform and thereafter, the efforts that are being made to remedy the situation in their favour by NGOs and the overall experience of Sathi in reuniting these children with their families.

The policies, rules and regulations on child protection relevant for such children on railway platforms are examined in the next chapter. Bodies, such as National Commission for Protection of Child Rights and the district-level Child Welfare Committees and Government Children's Homes, are described. The gap between resources available and the needs of children is highlighted.

In the next few chapters we present from children's point of view the stories of arriving on the platforms and moving through the shelters, government homes and ultimately succeeding in finding their way back to their families. The efforts made by staff of NGOs like Sathi to identify, rescue and reunite them with their families or send them to appropriate institutions are also detailed. These narratives are based on the cases and records of Sathi and some field interviews.

The third chapter describes a typical day on a railway platform and the feelings of children as they arrive. Staff on platform duty has a tough routine. They have to develop and build rapport with potential allies like the police and vendors and be on guard against others who may be interested in grabbing new arrivals (such as child traffickers and the older children's platform gangs).

The fourth chapter presents the typical routine in a Sathi shelter which is an open shelter that hosts children till they can return home or be sent to appropriate alternative locations. Children get basic needs and a caring, friendly place to relax in. As they unwind, they choose how much to divulge about themselves. The staff is watchful but gentle throughout and counsellors are available to talk at length with each child.

In the fifth chapter, the actual working of a Child Welfare Committee (CWC) is described through the children's eyes, based on our direct observations and research reports available in Sathi. The experiences of children in government homes are also described. There are many issues that children face in these homes which are presented from their perspective.

The sixth chapter presents an overview of a camp with focus on family reintegration. The boys settle down to deeper reflection on their choices and opportunities and most of them are glad to retrace their steps and return to a more orderly and settled life. A variety of inputs are skillfully interwoven to create the atmosphere for calming the children. These are described from the children's eyes.

The seventh chapter is on the theme of homecoming and the tumult that this generates in the whole village or neighbourhood. The relief and joy of parents and the deep satisfaction that the Sathi team derives from these reunions is also presented. Many small steps that together add up and help the child to 'live happily ever after' are presented here.

The eighth chapter reverts to the larger panorama and describes Sathi's efforts to build partnerships and collaboration to take their work forward. It concludes by summarising all the arguments for and against the different options like family reunification.

The ninth chapter uses the Hart framework of children's participation to study the range of interventions developed by the NGO sector to address these issues. The challenges of balancing between the current comfort of the child and the skills required for the future have been addressed in many creative ways by various NGOs and these ideas and efforts are presented in the chapter. They are also compared in terms of the rungs on the participation ladder.

The tenth chapter brings in international comparisons of how the issues are dealt with in more developed or better administered systems. It highlights options now favoured, such as fostering and the redesign of institutional care systems to create more of a family atmosphere.

We conclude with the eleventh chapter which offers an analyses the future directions Sathi may wish to take in the emerging scenario. An annexure provides the history of Sathi over the last two decades.

We have tried to keep notes and references to the minimum. Our main sources of information are the reports and research of Sathi and our own research both in the field and online.

If you are a reader interested in the larger picture, then you may prefer to read the first, second, ninth, tenth and eleventh chapters. If you are drawn to the book because you deeply care about the lives of these vulnerable children you will wish to dwell on the third, fourth, fifth, sixth, seventh and eighth chapters. We strongly recommend that you break your pattern and read the other bit as carefully as you read your preferred bit, or read the whole book carefully (in short).

The issue at hand needs both your head and your heart. This has prompted us to keep the children's experiences in the forefront throughout the book. We hope that on reading this you will actively look for opportunities to include family reunion as a serious option in any intervention or activity you may wish to take up.

Acknowledgements

We present an overview of the lives of India's railway children, mostly adolescent boys, who leave their families, often over trivial arguments, to arrive on railway platforms which then become their homes.

The work has been challenging and rewarding especially because we are not experts in the child rights domain of social work. We would like to acknowledge the support we have received from many sources.

Our first 'thank you' goes to Mr Pramod Kulkarni, Secretary and Founder of Sathi, whom we both have admired over many years, for trusting us to write about Sathi.

Many children and their families came forward to share their personal and at times painful stories with us. These conversations and meetings brought home to us the complexity of Sathi's task. We are very grateful to all of them.

As part of our research we visited many NGOs working for children in need of care and protection. They received us graciously and took time to highlight the nuances of their work, and how they view the whole question of runaway boys and family reunions.

We were also able to meet the officials and administrators who manage government homes for children and understand how that system works. Railway officials and railway police (RPF and GRP) gave us their time and described how they see the issue of children on the platform. CWC members were kind enough to permit us to observe their proceedings. Ms Neena Nayak, then with the Karnataka state Child Protection Committee, offered us her perspectives when we started this work. We met representatives of several donor agencies, both Indian and international, to understand how they locate Sathi's efforts in the spectrum of services needed for vulnerable children in India. All these people helped us a lot in getting the big picture. We thank all of them for making the time for us and sharing their views freely.

Mr Basavaraj Shali, Deputy Secretary in Sathi and Ms Savita Shastri, Programme Manager, organised all the background work for us and kept us supplied continuously with valuable information. Sathi managers, such as Mr Manoj and Mr Dikunath, were very resourceful in helping us with the field visits. Their support made it possible to finish the work on time.

Ms Kate Bulman came to our rescue when we wanted to present the situation in the UK as a counterpoint to India. She was able to persuade a young person to contribute her first-person account comparing her life in a government institution and a foster home. We thank both Ms Bulman and the young lady for their timely contributions.

Mahalakshmi Sundaraman helped us with the background research on the policies and the government's initiatives for child protection. More importantly, she edited our rough writing to improve the readability and cohesion of a book by two people who write very differently. We are very grateful both for her enthusiasm and her interest in the topic as well as her professional support. Surya Jyothi Murali also supported us with the documentation and we are grateful for her help.

This being a book about families we naturally turned to young people in our families for support. Kripa Venkatesh (Lalitha's niece) and May Bulman (Malcom's granddaughter) were kind enough to be our 'test' readers for early versions of our chapters and offered us insightful comments suggestion to improve clarity. We are very thankful to the young ladies for the specific feedback and loving encouragement.

SAGE Publications has been supportive and we thank them for agreeing to publish the work. Vivek Mehra, MD and CEO, took special interest in seeing the book through. We received support and encouragement from Rekha Natarajan and Neelakshi Chakraborty, who were with SAGE earlier. R Chandrashekar and Shreya Lall are the current team members we worked closely with to complete the project. We gratefully acknowledge all their support. We also record our thanks to an external referee (unnamed) who has encouraged us with a positive report.

Kripa's comment when she read the early draft was 'I wanted to make a change when I read the chapters and hopefully everyone else who reads the book will feel that way as well'. This is indeed the purpose of our writing. We hope to bring our readers closer to the children we are writing about, taking them beyond the numbers and the macro-picture. We take full responsibility for the shortcomings which remain and look forward to debating and dialoguing on all the issues we have raised.

Chapter One

India's Railway Children

The Children We Are Writing About

This book is about children. It is not about all children, but about those children in India who for some reason leave their homes and families, usually by their own choice. The phenomenon of 'runaway children', as it is loosely called, is global. Wherever there are families with children, there are some children who choose to go away from home. The last official estimate on the numbers of street children across India was 11,000,000. It is estimated that across 50 main railway stations, at least 70,000 and perhaps upto 120,000 (alone or unaccompanied by family) arrive onto the platforms every year. In comparison, it is estimated that about 84,000 children do this every year in the UK.

It is likely that more children take this step in India than in any other country simply because India is home to the largest number of children in the world. China has about 12 per cent more people in total, but India has about one third more under 18-year-olds. India is also home to a very large number of very poor people. Poverty is by no means the only reason why children run away from home, but it does play an important part.

This book is not about all runaway children in India. It is focused on Indian children who have used trains to take them away from home, and who live on railway station platforms or on trains. It is not known whether these children make up the largest proportion of Indian runaways, but there are certainly very many of them, and they are relatively easy to identify in the confined space of a railway station. Their situation is probably no worse or better than that of the hundreds of thousands of other children who live on India's city streets.

There are many different terms for runaway children, or for what they become once they have successfully run away from their homes. Many live on the street, and are called street children. But in India and a few other countries, where railways provide the main form of long distance transport, there are large numbers of children who live on railway station platforms, or on trains themselves. They are known as railway children. Bus stations also provide homes and livelihood for large numbers of children.

This book presents the issues and challenges of reaching out to these 'railway children', particularly through the experiences of Sathi, an NGO based in Bangalore. This organisation has chosen to work with children on railway platforms across India with the intention of reuniting them with families where ever possible.

There are a number of books, feature films, documentaries and studies about runaway children themselves, and about 'street children', since so many runaways end up living on the streets. Some of these present sad cases, perhaps with some analysis. Others, like the film *Slumdog Millionaire*, offer some hope of the children succeeding spectacularly, despite terrible ordeals. They all remind us of the problem which we may tend to ignore because it is so widespread and so complex. Besides, when we come across such children we think they are usually a nuisance, or even a threat.

This book is different. It includes a number of such stories, most with sad beginnings and some with happy endings. However, the focus of the book, and indeed our reason for writing it, is the way in which one institution, Sathi, is trying to deal with the problem. The purpose of the stories is to show how complex the problem can be, and demonstrate the failures and successes of those who try to deal with it.

What Can Be Done with These Runaways?

Fundamentally, there are three ways in which society can try to deal with runaway children. We can ignore them, find new homes for them, or send them back to their own homes. In practice, we do all three of these things. Sathi concentrates very much on the third option—sending them home—but we should look briefly at all three options before we describe Sathi's work in more detail in the remainder of the book.

First, and most simply, we can leave runaway children alone, ignore them. This may seem inhuman, or even outrageous, but we have to accept that there are millions of such children on the streets and railway platforms of India and elsewhere, in spite of all the effort that goes into preventing them from being there. It could even be argued that all the efforts of Sathi and the many other institutions which try to solve the problem do not achieve very much. The end result, in terms of the numbers and condition of the children, is perhaps not very different from what would be the case if nothing was being done about the problem, or even if it was not treated as a problem at all.

Let us examine two brief examples of how such a 'laissez-faire' policy can work out (Box 1.1).

Box 1.1: *Amit's Platform Life*

Amit Das had been abandoned on a railway platform and grew up in Howrah station in Calcutta. He doesn't remember who his parents were or where he came from. He is now 15, and has made the platform his home. He is notorious for stealing, and he has no fear of the police or punishment. He boasts that he has been in custody nine or 10 times, and he has become a hard-core drug addict. All the money he earns is spent on food, entertainment and drugs.

Source: Don Bosco Ashalayam (2005).

This sad story is true, and all too frequent. This is why we feel concerned for the children whom we encounter on the streets and platforms, and why we try to 'rescue' them from such a sad existence, and to protect ourselves from the harm that they might cause us.

Such an outcome is not inevitable, however. Even a neglected runaway can emerge successfully from the experience and repay society many times over for the discomfort he might have caused. Like so many social interventions, it is impossible to assess the overall impact of what is done (see Box 1.2).

There are no statistics to show trends in the number of children who run away from home. Are there more of them running away now than there were 20 years ago? Are more of those who do run away more successfully 'rescued' from the streets or railway platforms where they live? We do not really know. It is possible that the social and economic pressures that lead children to run away from home, such as urbanisation and weakening family ties, are such that far more children than before are taking this step. Even if the numbers are increasing, perhaps many more

---

Box 1.2: *Charlie Chaplin's Tough Childhood*

Charles Spencer Chaplin was born in a poor district of London in 1889. His mother, Hannah a talented singer, actress and piano player, spent most of her life in and out of mental hospitals. His father, Charles Spencer Chaplin, Sr, was a fairly successful singer until he began drinking. After his parents separated, Charlie and his half-brother, Sidney, spent most of their childhood in orphanages, where they often went hungry and were beaten if they misbehaved. Charlie was thrown on his own resources before he reached the age of 10 as the early death of his father and the subsequent illness of his mother made it necessary for Charlie and his brother, Sidney, to fend for themselves. Having inherited natural talents from their parents, the youngsters took to the stage as the best opportunity for a career. Barely able to read and write, Chaplin left school to tour with a group of comic entertainers. Later he starred in a comedy act. When he was about 12, he got his first chance to act in a legitimate stage show, *Sherlock Holmes*. At the close of this engagement, Charlie started a career as a comedian in Vaudeville. By the age of 19 he had become one of the most popular music-hall performers in England and he eventually went to the USA in 1910. The rest, as they say, is history.

would have run away and stayed away had there been no effort to reach out to them.

It is not in the nature of humanity, however, to neglect problems of this kind. Even if our efforts fail, we keep trying, often without changing the ways we address the problem. Many agencies have been working in this field and nearly all of them profess to believe that returning home in the right circumstances is the best outcome for a child who has run away. They differ very widely in their definition of what these right circumstances are. Many organisations, including both governmental and non-governmental agencies, focus their main attention on the provision of safe, decent and child-friendly institutions where runaway children can be accommodated, in the short, medium or long term. Such institutions or other alternatives such as providing foster parents are necessary when a child's natural home either does not exist, or is manifestly unsuitable. There is, however, a danger that their staff and management may develop a vested interest in filling their institutions, rather than trying in every way to restore children to their homes. Episodes of abuse and harsh treatment of children in such institutions are unfortunately common across the globe. Like any other remedy for a social problem, or indeed a problem of any kind, institutionalisation, or being kept in such an institution, can have good or bad results. The borderline between a prison and a hostel is not clear. The children have to be locked up to stop them from running away again, and children who have deliberately chosen the freedom of the railways or the streets over their home lives are all too likely to regard being locked up in an institution as even being worse than their homes. They run away again, at the first opportunity, particularly, of course, if the obvious intention of whoever has taken them there is to send them back to the parental homes from which they have run away (Boxes 1.3 and 1.4).

The word 'institutionalisation' has a bad sound about it; someone who has been 'institutionalised' is automatically assumed to have been damaged rather than benefitted from the experience, and many institutions undoubtedly do more harm than good to the children who live in them. As with all the options, however, the outcome need not be a disaster (see Box 1.5).

Box 1.3: *A Victim or a Villain?*

Clyde Barrow, the notorious 1930s outlaw, was born into a poor family in America and had run away from home in his early years. He was arrested when he was 17 for stealing a car. The second time he was arrested was for being in possession of stolen goods. Undeterred, he went on to become a bank robber. While serving his prison sentence for this, he was repeatedly sexually assaulted by another inmate. Clyde broke the inmate's skull—this was his first murder. It is believed that Barrow did not want to gain fame by robbing and looting but wanted to revenge himself against the Texas prison system for the abuses which were heaped on him while he served his sentence. He met with a sad end when he was ambushed by the police.

Source: FBI (2013) and Wikipedia (2013a).

Box 1.4: *Dangers of a Runaway's Life*

Films have succeeded in presenting the hard realities of street children's lives and positively influencing social attitudes towards these children and their plight. The depth of the trap is best understood when we look into the stories of the child artistes in these films.

Fernando Ramos da Silva, a working-class boy in San Paulo, was only 11 when director Hector Babenco cast him in the title role of *Pixote* (1980), a haunting film about children forced to become street criminals. The movie highlighted the issue and won much acclaim and Fernando became an instant international celebrity. Sadly, his fame and success were fleeting. He suffered a severe identity crisis and was subjected to humiliation at home. In 1987, he was caught in a police raid, sent to prison and eventually killed.

When Mira Nair made *Salaam Bombay* in 1989, she was very aware of the Pixote tragedy. Two decades later, Mira is proud of what Hansa and Shafiq, the main actors in the film, have done with their lives. She adds:

> Hansa and Shafiq are very content and happily married. Shafiq is a sound recordist and an auto rickshaw owner. I was very particular about their lives. When the child actor from Pixote, a film that deeply inspired me, passed away, I was devastated. We realised the danger of working with street kids in Salaam Bombay to portray their own lives. When we couldn't find institutions to support these

(Box 1.4 contd)

(Box 1.4 contd)

kids, we created our own institution, the Salaam Baalak Trust. Many kids who acted in *Salaam Bombay* worked at the centres formed by our Trust and then went on to do other things in life.

Luck played an important role in Shafiq's life when, as a clueless 12-year old, he landed the role of 'Krishna' in *Salaam Bombay*. He had run away from his home in Bangalore to Bombay 'just for fun'. He survived off the streets making a few friends. One day a lady approached them with an offer to be a part of a drama club which provided one meal and paid Rs 20 for a day. This turned out to be the talent hunt for the film. Its success earned Shafiq a national award for best child artist in 1988. He returned to Bangalore and struggled as a camera assistant before ultimately becoming an auto driver in order to make ends meet.

Source: Wikipedia (2013b).

Box 1.5: *Transformations*

Vivek, a 14-year-old, dropped out of school and joined a gang of teenage thieves in Chikballapur, a small town near Bangalore. The police caught him in 2007 and he was sent to the official Observation Home for Juveniles in Bangalore. The Juvenile Justice Board released him and sent him back to the custody of his parents. They brought him to ECHO, a non-government institution in Bangalore, for rehabilitation. At ECHO, Vivek settled in and began his studies. He now works in a retail Bata foot-wear shop and earns Rs 4,500 (US$ 100) a month. He is also pursuing a Bachelors degree. Vivek is a talented actor and dancer and he often appears in plays organised by ECHO (ECHO Souvenir 2000–10).

Ivian Sarcos lost her parents at a very young age and was institutionalised for five years in a nunnery. She dreamed that she might one day become a nun. But things changed when she gained a degree in human resource management and got a job in a broadcasting company. She became a fashion model and was eventually crowned Miss World 2011 in London. On winning the award, Ivian said that she wanted to use her fame to work with orphans like she herself had been, and with troubled teenagers such as she might have become. She has gone on to do exactly that.

Source: Story gathered in the course of our field visit to ECHO (2013). On Ivian Sarcose, Wikipedia (2013c).

There are large numbers of governmental and non-governmental agencies which work to address the problem of runaway children, for the sake of society at large, of the children themselves and their parents. Many of them, including Sathi itself, provide temporary or in some cases permanent alternative homes for children who have run away. Others attempt to find new homes for the children through fostering or adoption. These methods are not as yet widely used in India, but they have more or less supplanted institutional residential homes in many wealthier countries. In India, children who run away from home, and who are 'caught' or 'rescued', depending on one's point of view, are more often kept in long term institutional care.

Sathi uses a number of approaches to reunite runaway children with their families, depending on how long the child has been away from home and the nature of the problems which induced him to run away. These include working with the parents as well as with the child. Sathi's own shelter homes are designed to accommodate children only for a few days. If Sathi cannot send a child home, in spite of its best efforts, the child can be sent through the official channels to an existing governmental or non-governmental children's institution. As we shall see, Sathi also works intensively and very successfully with children who are in such institutions and tries to get them to go home, regardless of whether they have been sent to the institution by Sathi or from elsewhere.

The most obvious solution is to send runaway children back to where they came from: their homes. Or, better still, but in general beyond the scope of this book, or of Sathi and the other institutions that deal with runaways, to stop them running away in the first place. Institutions such as Sathi and others try to discourage the children whom they have sent home from running away again, by addressing whatever problems that may have caused them to want to leave. However, genuine prevention, stopping or reducing of the scale of the problem before it happens, falls into the purview of social work, poverty alleviation, family counselling and all manner of similar interventions.

Some children's welfare institutions, such as the Association for Promoting Social Action (APSA) in Bangalore, have identified the parts of the city where most of the street children with whom they work have come from, and attempt to work in these areas to reduce the numbers who run away. This is difficult even in one city, but the children whom Sathi meets at railway stations have come from all over India, and even from neighbouring countries such as Nepal and Bangladesh. Sathi has comprehensive data on all the many thousands of children for whom it has worked. So far it has not been possible to identify particular villages or urban areas from which large numbers run away, and to attempt to work there in order to tackle the problem at its source. Therefore, for the present, the focus of Sathi's work, and of this book, is on helping children who have run away, to return to their homes.

Family Reunification

It should be obvious already that it is not easy to send a child home, or to ensure that he or she remains at home once he has been taken there. Many, if not most, children do not want to go home when first approached by welfare staff. They may be unwilling or unable to say where their homes are. Their homes may be hundreds or thousands of kilometres away from where they have been 'caught', or in places where people speak different languages or in urban slums or rural villages where written addresses are unknown. In some cases, parents, if there are any, may not want these children back.

These are the obstacles that Sathi has to overcome, and it is much easier in the short term, to adopt the institutionalisation option, under which all the children can be treated the same. The book will describe the ways in which Sathi undertakes the more complex but in the long term less expensive and socially more desirable task of reuniting children with their families. However, it is important to be clear from the outset that the outcome is not always successful (Box 1.6).

Sathi estimates that after the complex and quite lengthy process—which will be described in this book—between 90 and 95 per cent of the children whom they have taken home stay at

> **Box 1.6:** *A Rolling Stone*
>
> Twelve-year-old Baba Fakruddin has run away from home six times. His mother works in Saudi Arabia as a maid and his father has abandoned the family. He stayed with his grandparents for a brief while before running away. Sathi rescued him and tried to send the boy back to his grandparents. But his grandparents refused to take him back. He was admitted at Anugraha for basic education and he ran away from there too. His whereabouts are unknown.
>
> *Source:* Sathi Annual Report (2010–2011).

home thereafter, for as long as children in general stay at home. The remaining are failures; perhaps not as dramatic or sad as this last case, but still failures. The overriding objective is to make the process more effective, that is, to improve the success rate, and at the same time more efficient, that is, to reduce the time and cost that it requires. The following cases (see Box 1.7) are typical of the way in which most of Sathi's cases turn out, and of what should be result for every child (Box 1.7).

How Many Children Are on Railway Platforms?

It is of course impossible to accurately assess how many children run away or measure the scale of the problem which Sathi is attempting to address. Many children run away and are never contacted by NGOs such as Sathi, or by the police or other authorities, and many of these no doubt return home, some within a few days and others perhaps after much longer periods. Some recent measures to set up a missing children's information exchange are still in the initial stages. There are all manner of estimates of the numbers of children in India who run away, or are living on the streets or on railway platforms, or are 'in care' of various kinds. Because India as a country has the largest population of children in the world and poverty is widespread, the numbers are frightening. Jaimala Hitesh (Director, Vatsalya,

Box 1.7: *Home, Sweet Home*

Sahil was 13 when he stole a small amount of gold jewellery from his parents in Kumte village in Korregaon, 200 kilometres from Mumbai in Maharashtra. He ran away from home for fear of being caught, boarded a train, and soon fell into bad company with some other railway boys and became a drug addict at a very young age. The police rescued the boy from a railway station and sent him to a Government Children's Home. He stayed there for two years and then ran away again. Sathi staff found him at Pune station. He was sent to a Sathi rehabilitation camp to overcome his drug addiction. At the end of the camp, Sahil resolved that he would change for the better and said he wanted to go home. Sathi reunited him with his mother and Sahil has gone back to school and is continuing his studies.

Ravi, a 16-year-old boy from Raichur, Karnataka, ran away from home because he was forced to do household chores. He stayed on the Raichur railway platform for 10 days and did menial jobs for a living. He also got addicted to *beedi* and *gutka*. He was rescued by Sathi and brought to their local shelter near the station. The staff at the Sathi centre counselled him and motivated him to return home. Eight years later, Sathi staff visited the child's home to check on his progress. Ravi has a good job in a local agency for bottled gas and is earning Rs 3,500 a month. He is married with two children and supports his family.

The child's growth after home placement: Ravi is now 24 years old and at present he is working at a gas service center. He earns Rs. 3500 per month and gives the entire amount to his family. He is attending evening classes and studying for 10th exam. He is more motivated towards completing his education. He is having a healthy relationship with the family members.

Happy outcome of a child who is picked up in very difficult circumstances by Sathi, is taken to a camp, home is identified, is happily reunited with his parents and 'lives happily ever after'

Source: Sahil's example: Sathi Annual Report (2006–07) and Ravi's example Sathi (2011) Annual Report 2010–2011.

Jaipur) says there are 18,000,000 street children in the country, which presumably includes those who live and work on railway platforms. In 2006, UNICEF estimated that there are 11,000,000 such children in India. The official document 'India: Third and Fourth Combined Periodic Report on the Convention on the

Rights of the Child' released in October 2011 by the Ministry of Women and Child Development of the Government of India refrains from stating a number and acknowledges the lack of reliable data. The broad differences may result as much from the use of different definitions as from the difficulty of counting, but it is clear that there are very large numbers of such children, and that they constitute a problem, to themselves, to their families and to society in general.

In a 2005 study of children who worked on eight large railway stations in northern India between Delhi and Bhopal, Plan International found that there were almost 700 children working in the eight stations. About half of them were living at home in neighbouring slums, and came to the station every day for work, and most of the other half lived day and night in the station itself. A few were staying in government or voluntary organisations' shelters near their respective stations. Of these, 40 per cent had been working on the platforms for over a year. The children reported that they were only able to remain on the platforms where they obtained their livelihood by submitting to the railway police personnel's demands for a share of their takings, or free services, and they were nevertheless all too frequently beaten and otherwise abused. There are 158 so-called 'important stations' in the Indian railways system. If the average figure of about 40 children residing in each of these stations is assumed to be typical, the total number of children who live more or less permanently on India's railway stations will come to something over 6,000. This figure is of course for working children, and is unlikely to include children who have just arrived at a station after having left home elsewhere.

A later publication from Childline in 2007 stated that its offices had received phone calls reporting between 40,000 and 45,000 missing children every year, between 1996 and 2001. Many children used the railways to runaway and to stay away too. The proportion of such children who were eventually traced varied widely, from as high as 99 per cent in the state of Gujarat, one of India's better-off states, to as low as 22 per cent in Orissa, the poorest state. These figures do not of course include every missing child; Bihar, the state from which a large number of Sathi's children have originated, did not have a child line service at the time of this report. An increasing number of such children, and their families, are now starting to use the nation-wide 'Childline' system, which offers 24/7 telephone services, guaranteed to be answered in three rings or less. The runaway children and their families can use this service to report their whereabouts or about missing children, respectively. The numbers may be expected to have increased in recent years as knowledge of the Childline service and mobile telephone ownership and use have increased.

Why Do Runaway Children Use the Railways?

The railways occupy a very special place in India, not only in the economy but also culturally. For the last 100 or more years, the railways have been the dominant form of long-distance transport. If you want to get away, to be free, to see life beyond the narrow confines of a small community, or merely to hide and disappear into the masses of India, you take the train. There is no data on the means children use to leave home, but it seems likely that most use the train. It is not easy to enter a bus unseen, or to hide once you have got on, but railway stations and trains themselves are relatively open. Ticket collectors cannot cover everyone, least of all small people in crowded unreserved coaches, and they certainly cannot search under every seat. What is more, the train provides more than transport; it can itself provide a livelihood. Small people can quickly fit into the informal mobile economy of a train. They can steal, or beg, or sing songs or dance, or they can assist the official vendors, in return for a scrap to eat or a little change. Some children can even make a semi-permanent living on these trains. Trains are thus a means of transport, and a possible source of livelihood.

Children are also relatively secure. They are sheltered from the worst of the weather, there is water to drink and children are less likely to be physically abused on a train than on the street. In some sense, a train offers an ideal combination of the basic facilities which a child needs to move, and to survive. The railway station is an extension of the train. It is not a public place. People on platforms should in theory have tickets to travel or platform tickets. In addition to basic services, there are many opportunities for informal livelihoods. And, if a child left home by train, it is the point of arrival, as well as the point of departure to another place when life gets too tough, or too boring. The platform is thus an obvious place for runaway children to choose.

Runaway children are more visible on a platform than on a street; exploitation is easier to identify in the semi-protected environment of a railway station than the urban jungle. A child on a platform who is helping a platform vendor, or is being 'sold' for sexual services, can more easily be identified, and assisted, than one on the street. Thus the choice of the station platform is a very good option for those setting out to work with runaways in India.

This does not mean that life on the platform is a desirable or happy situation. Khushboo Jain, a researcher, became concerned with the plight of the children she saw in the railway stations of Delhi and filed a suit against the Ministry of Railways in the High Court of Delhi in 2012 . The court's orders in February 2013 place a great deal of responsibility on the Station Master and the Railway Police. All efforts are to be made to trace the family and produce children before the CWCs or similar body within 24 hours of their being found. Adequate records will be maintained about the children found and girls and boys are to be cared for separately. Information on such children must be published in local and national newspapers and on the railway portal so that families can trace them easily (Das, 2013).

Inflow of Children

The importance of this issue becomes sharper when we consider estimates of the daily arrivals of runaway children on railway platforms in some of India's main cities, and the number of children whom any traveller can see, who live and work on the platform. These are based on actual surveys (see Table 1.1) conducted by Sathi and partner NGOs over a small period in each of these

Table 1.1:
Estimates of Unaccompanied Children Arriving on Platforms

	Platforms Covered in 2013	Arrivals per Annum	Children Living on Platforms
1	Bangalore City	2,200	3
2	Yeshwantpur	1,825	2
3	Old Delhi	3,650	35
4	New Delhi	9,125	50
5	Katihar	1,095	35
6	Gaya	730	12
7	Kanpur	1,460	30
8	Lucknow	1,095	15
9	Mughalserai	1,460	30
10	Gorakhpur	1,825	35
11	Pune	1,825	30
	Total	26,290	277

Source: Sathi Annual Report 2013, Chapter 1.

stations within the last three years. The daily arrival numbers for these 11 stations add up to 230 children a day, or well over 80,000 children a year, whereas 'only' 277 children, or roughly one day's arrivals, remain on the platform. This shows all too clearly that a large number of children come to the stations and just melt into the large cities finding work and shelter wherever they can. This underlines the importance of reaching children as soon as they arrive and highlights the scale of the issue.

The survey data in Table 1.1 shows that there are all too many children arriving on platforms who need help.

Sathi's Efforts

Sathi is an NGO whose work is mainly based on railway station platforms and it has stayed firmly committed to this location. Nevertheless, it is clear that Sathi's achievement in getting some

35,000 children to go back home in the last 20 years, and continuing to repatriate over 6,000 every year, some 90 per cent of whom do not run away again, is more than the proverbial 'drop in the bucket'.

Newly arrived children are not sure where to go; they may do their best to appear confident, but Sathi's staff have learned how to identify them. The longer they have been away from home, the harder it is to get them back. There are small gangs of long-term residents on most large railway stations, but Sathi has found that most unaccompanied children are recent arrivals. Hence, they are more likely to be able to send them home successfully.

Sathi has developed and is continually improving a clear system for dealing with such numbers. Unusually for voluntary agencies working in such a highly emotive and sensitive field, Sathi methodically documents its achievements, including its failures; these findings occupy many reports, but the overall system, and its results, are briefly summarised in Figure 1.1. This shows the average results achieved with hundred children who are contacted by Sathi on a railway platform.

This shows that only 50 out of a 100 children with whom Sathi makes an initial contact go home and stay there. This may appear to be a poor result for an institution which is so firmly focussed on getting children to go home, and to stay there, but Figure 1.1 graphically demonstrates how many hurdles have to be overcome between the initial contact and successful return home.

Initially, and not unexpectedly, 20 children 'slip out' of Sathi's care during the few minutes that elapse between their first contact with a Sathi staff member and their arrival at the Sathi shelter, which is usually within a short walk of the railway station where the child was first contacted. The children have run away from home, usually quite recently, and they are all too aware that both their families and society at large disapprove of such behaviour. They may also be aware of other dangers through children's own informal information channels, and perhaps from their families too, of the risk of being kidnapped or trafficked. A newly arrived child, therefore, views any adult, however kind and considerate she or he might appear to be, either as an 'official' who intends to make you go home, or as a trafficker who wants to exploit

Figure 1.1:
A Profile of Sathi's Efforts (2006–2009)

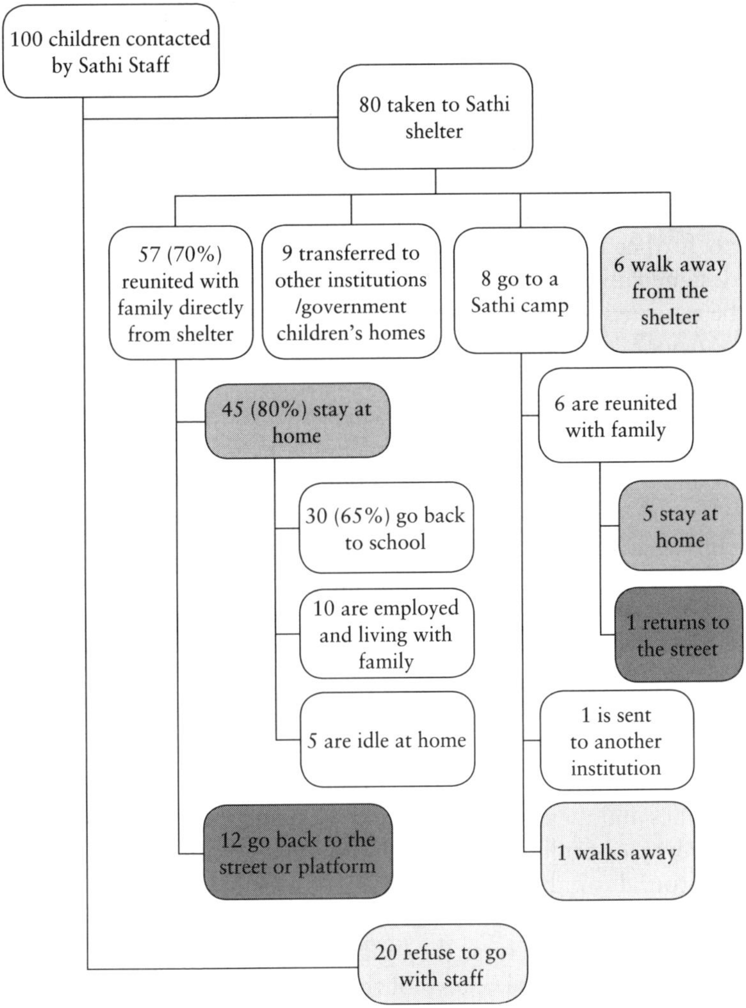

100 children contacted by Sathi Staff

80 taken to Sathi shelter

57 (70%) reunited with family directly from shelter

9 transferred to other institutions /government children's homes

8 go to a Sathi camp

6 walk away from the shelter

45 (80%) stay at home

6 are reunited with family

30 (65%) go back to school

5 stay at home

10 are employed and living with family

1 returns to the street

5 are idle at home

1 is sent to another institution

12 go back to the street or platform

1 walks away

20 refuse to go with staff

Source: Mathani (2009).

you. The staff members have to overcome all these quite rational fears, and by their efforts, persuade a child to go with them. At times they are interrupted by other passengers who believe that they may be trying to kidnap or traffic the child. In these circumstances, and in spite of all these problems, it is extraordinary, and creditable, that the Sathi platform staff succeeds in persuading 80 of the children who they contact on platforms come with them to the nearby shelter.

Fifty-seven children (70 per cent of those who do agree to go to the Sathi shelter) are successfully returned home within a few days. This is the first point at which Sathi's philosophy and focus is implemented in practice, and the achievement of this result would in itself be remarkable, even if the remaining children had no further contact with Sathi. As Figure 1.1 shows, Sathi has designed an array of methods to help those children who cannot be returned home soon after the initial contact.

About 23 (30 per cent) children who have come from the railway platforms to the Sathi shelters cannot be returned home at once. They may have no idea where their homes are. Sathi staff has developed a range of very ingenious techniques and questions to find out where children have come from. Even if they do know where they have come from, or Sathi can find out, there are of course cases when a child should not go home. They may have been assaulted or abused, their families may have driven them out, or they may not have any family at all. Sathi estimates that over two-thirds of the runaway children whom they meet have left home for trivial reasons, such as are described later in this book, but the other third have more serious problems. These do not necessarily mean that the children should never return home. Family reunion is possible perhaps after some counselling for their families and themselves. The task of getting these children home, however, or finding another solution, takes more time and effort.

Around a half of these 'difficult' cases are referred to other institutions run by government, or by NGOs. If they are left to fend for themselves, they may get rapidly 'seduced' by the freedom and new pleasures of the street or the platform so that they do not want to go home. In general, the longer a child is away from home the more difficult it is to get him or her back. Sathi tries to minimise the delay but at the same time offers the necessary to support and do whatever is essential to find a child's home, secure his/her willingness to go home and the family's agreement to take him/her. The compromise is not easy.

The main instrument that Sathi uses in these cases is the three to four weeks' camp. This is the key ingredient in Sathi's strategy, for dealing with children who cannot be taken home within a few days. It involves taking 20 or so children to a quiet and isolated calm place, and putting them through a carefully designed routine of games, lessons, and individual and group counselling. As a result of this, as the diagram shows, three-quarters of the children who have attended the camp go home. Given that nearly all of these are children who would or could not go home when Sathi first contacted them, this is not an unsatisfactory outcome. In the last three years, this analysis has helped to improve the quality of family reunification and these efforts have led to an improvement in the percentage of children who continue with the family. Almost 95 per cent of the children reunited through early intervention continue with the family and 90 per cent of those reunited through camps continue as well.

This analysis has helped Sathi to bring about further improvements in processes. Work in the government children's homes has spread rapidly too and the picture over the last five years has changed significantly as the analysis for 2013 reveals (Figure 1.2). Sathi is now able to reunite 68 per cent of the children contacted. The number who walk away after reaching the shelter has been reduced sharply (less than 1 per cent).

Sathi also attempts to follow up its work, through surveys to find out whether children whom it has helped to return home remain at home, or run away again (Table 1.2).

It is remarkable that less than 5 per cent of the children promptly restored to their families leave home again. When they are restored after along separation from government homes and through camps 12 per cent are not traceable again. If the results from this survey are extrapolated over 60 per cent return to school. A further 20 per cent go to work; this is not necessarily child labour since the majority are over 14 years of age by the time they have been returned home. A similar number stay at home though idle.

Words like 'escape' implies that the children in the Sathi shelter or a government or NGO children's institution are prisoners—that they cannot come and go as they wish. This is true of a few

Figure 1.2:
Profile of Sathi's Efforts (2013)

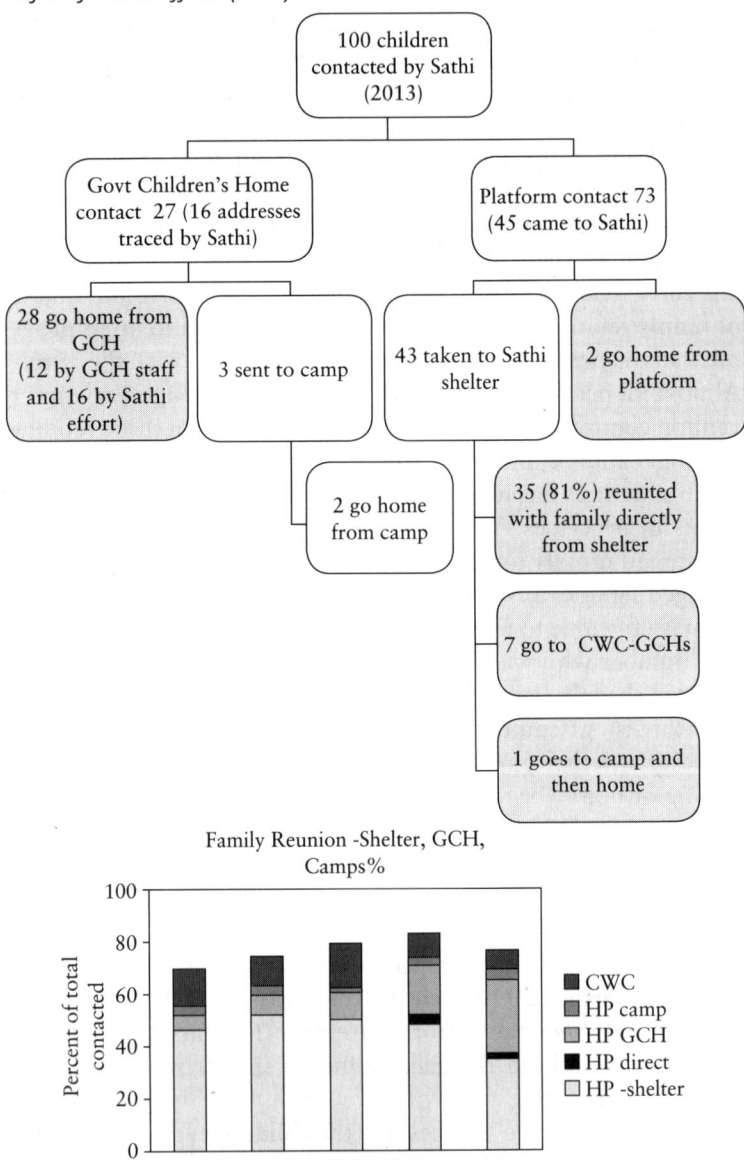

Source: Sathi Annual Report (2013, chapter 1).

Table 1.2:
Telephone Follow Up 2010–2013

Homeplaced through →	Shelter	GCH HP*	Camps
Total no. contacted	10,578	2,659	685
No. at home	10,191	2,333	604
Percent at home	96	88	88
No. in school	6,450	1,012	255
Percent at school	63	43	42
No. working	1,941	631	145
Percent at work	19	27	24
No. idle	1,792	685	204
Percent idle	18	29	34

Source: Compilation from Sathi Annual reports 2011 and 2013.
*GCH HP: Government Children's Homes Home-placed.

children's institutions, particularly government-run homes which accommodate children who are in conflict with the law. Sathi's own shelters are very modest and are far from secure. Sathi's staff feels quite strongly that the success of their approach depends on children's willingness to be part of the process. Children's grapevines are also quite effective; if it were known that the Sathi staff were taking children to locked shelters, the percentage of those whom Sathi contacts who then go willingly to the shelter would almost certainly be much reduced.

The figures that are given in the earlier diagram are unusual for any institution, in that they clearly include the numbers of children for whom Sathi's methods have not worked, who have walked away or have not gone home. One of the features which makes Sathi rather different is that it is managed like a business, with extensive records, and with clear and transparent cost information. Unlike many businesses, however, Sathi's reports and other documents contain as much information about failures as about successes. The management's concern is to share and develop new and better ways of helping runaway children, learning from what has gone wrong as well as from what goes right.

It is obviously difficult to allocate costs accurately to each component in the complex process of bringing a child home, but the cost of the simple and relatively short cycle of meeting a child on a railway platform and getting him or her home with only a week or so at most in a Sathi shelter is just over ₹3,000 (US$ 60). If this fast turnaround is not possible and the child has to go through the four weeks camp process, the cost increases to about ₹5,000 (US$ 100).

The costs of long term institutions vary, and the estimate of variable costs for keeping a child in a Government Home (where they should be housed according to the law) ranges from ₹30,000 (US$ 600) to ₹100,000 (US$ 2,000) per annum. Sathi's focus on getting children home therefore makes good economic as well as good human sense.

This book brings to you the adventures of children on India's railway platforms and the work and lives of those who meet and re-orient these children, gently pushing them back home or finding safer options acceptable to them.

References

Internet

Don Bosco Ashalayam. 2005. 'The vulnerability status of children living on the platforms of Howrah and Sealdah railway station', published by Don Bosco Ashalayam Documentation and Research Center, 158 Belilious Road, Kadamtala Howrah, Kolkata 2005. Pdf copy downloaded in April 2012 available with Dr Lalita Iyer http://www.ashalayam.org/Vulnerability%20status%20of%20 children%20living%20on%20train%20platforms.pdf) accessed on 6 April 2012.
Echo. 2013. retrieved from http://www.echoindia.org/tpap.html, Bangalore, accessed on 29-07-2013.
FBI. 2013. 'Clyde Barrow—Career in Crime', retrieved from http://www.fbi.gov/about-us/history/famous-cases/bonnie-and-clyde Washington, accessed on 29-07-2013.
Dr Rajshri Mathani, Tata Institute of Social Sciences.
Mathani, R. 2009. retrieved from http://www.sathiindia.org/sathi%20doc/Ourwork/ Conceptualization.ppt, Bangalore, 2009, accessed on 1 August 2013.
Wikipedia. 2013a. 'Bonnie and Clyde', retrieved from http://en.wikipedia.org/wiki/ Bonnie_and_Clyde, accessed on 29-07-2013.
Wikipedia. 2013b. 'Pixote' retrieved from http://en.wikipedia.org/wiki/Pixote, accessed on 27-07-2013.

http://www.railwaychildren.org.uk/frequently-asked-questions.asp.

Wikipedia. 2013c. 'Ivian Sarcose', retrieved from, http://en.wikipedia.org/wiki/ Ivian_Sarcos, accessed on 29-07-2013.

http://www.ashalayam.org/Vulnerability%20status%20of%20children%20 living%0on%20train%20platforms.pdf.

http://www.charliechaplin.com/en/biography/articles/21-Overview-of-His-Life.

http://www.notablebiographies.com/Ch-Co/Chaplin-Charlie.html.

http://www.mybangalore.com/article/life-after-salaam-bombay.html.

http://www.chetna-india.org/Pubs/Publication-Dreams%20on%20Wheeels-A%20 study%20on%20status%20of%20children%20.pdf.

Reports

ECHO. 2011. Souvenir (2000–2010), Bangalore 2011, p. 75.

Sathi. 2007. Annual Report 2006–2007, Bangalore 2007, p. 33

Sathi Annual Report. 2011. Annual Report (2010–2011), Bangalore, p. 72.

Sathi and Every Child UK. 2011. 'A Study to Understand and Enhance Learning on Rehabilitation and Social Integration of Children Home Placed Five Years Ago by Sathi.'

Ministry of Women and Child Development. 2011. 'India: Third and Fourth Combined Periodic Report on the Convention on the Rights of the Child.' Government of India: New Delhi.

Childline India Foundation. 2007. 'Missing Children of India, Issues and Approaches, A Childline Perspective.'

Sathi Annual Report 2013 Chapter 1.

Plan India, New Delhi 2005. 'Dreams on Wheels—A Situation Review of Children Living or Working on Eight Railway Stations from Hazrat Nizamuddin to Bhopal.'

UNICEF. 2006. 'State of the World's Children'.

Das, Udita. February 2013. Lost Childhoods, published by Paul Hamlyn Foundation, London, p. 44, www.phf.org.uk/downloaddoc.asp?id=931, accessed on 30-07-2013.

Book

Vatsalya. 2008. *Eighteen Million Question Marks: The Street Children of India.* Vatsalya: Jaipur.

Chapter Two

Conventions and Policies versus Practice and Reality

Good Intentions and How Far They Go

United Nations (UN) pronouncements are often very distant from reality, and although they may be phrased in the form of injunctions or even commands, with no emollient qualifiers such as 'best efforts' or 'when practical', there are few if any governments or societies which could claim that the UN or other international conventions in labour relations, the treatment of refugees, environmental protection or any other fields are obeyed to the letter.

Similarly, the gap between intentions and practice at the national level is often a very wide one, particularly in a country as large and as diverse as India. The effective distance between a UN agency in New York or Geneva and a government office in Delhi may be much less than the distance between Delhi and a rural village or even an urban slum or railway station within a few hundred metres of the office in Delhi itself.

The gaps between pronouncements and practices may be even wider in children's welfare than in other fields, because the subject is so emotive and any compromises in intentions seem so distasteful, and because actual practice is in homes and families rather than in institutions and is thus often unseen.

International Policies and Street Children

The UNICEF Convention on the Rights of the Child includes 54 articles and two optional protocols. It defines the rights of children, outlines the role of governments and emphasises the importance of the family's role in the upbringing of children. A number of articles in the Convention relate specifically to children who are separated from their parents, and to the respective rights of children themselves and of their parents, and thus to the issue of children who have gone away from home against the will of their parents.

Article 3 states categorically that 'the best interests of the child must be a top priority'; the use of the word 'a' as opposed to 'the' still leaves some room for doubt, but the emphasis of the Convention is on the rights of children themselves.

Article 5 refers to the necessity of 'respect[ing]' the rights as well as the responsibilities of parents.

Article 7 states that children have the right, 'as far as possible' to be cared for by their parents, and Article 9 says that they should not be separated from their parents unless this is in their best interests, such as in cases of abuse or neglect. Children should have the right to 'express their views', and these views should be 'taken seriously', but there is, not unreasonably, no direct implication that these views should prevail over those of their parents or of any other authority. The right of children to run away and to stay away if necessary is thus protected.

Article 20 specifically points out that governments should provide 'special protection and assistance' and 'alternative care' for any children who cannot or should for any reason not be allowed to stay at home.

Child Protection Law and Policy in India

The law in India for protection of children is within the ambit of Article 39 of the Constitution of India which commits the government to 'take all appropriate measures to promote physical and psychological recovery and social reintegration of a child victim of any form of neglect, exploitation, or abuse....Such recovery and reintegration shall take place in an environment which fosters the health, self-respect and dignity of the child.'

The Government of India does do this to an extent, as always through the mechanisms of the different states, and the level of provision tends to be inadequate in quantity and in quality. Here again, the reality of what can be seen every day at many railways stations and in many streets belies the intentions at the national level. It is clear that the Government of India, like most governments, is not completely able to fulfil what its own constitution enjoins it to do.

Article 39 also gives children the right 'to be protected from being abused and forced by economic necessity to enter occupations unsuited to their age or strength' and the right 'to equal opportunities and facilities to develop in a healthy manner and in conditions of freedom and dignity and guaranteed protection of childhood and youth against exploitation and against moral and material abandonment' (Wikipedia, 2013). Provisions of this sort which are so obviously flouted in practice, provide a set of standards to which institutions and individuals can appeal, and to which both government and civil society institutions such as Sathi can aspire.

The Children's Act of 1960 was the first Act in India to deal specifically with street children. It defined them as 'neglected' children, which included any child who was found to be homeless or without any means of subsistence or was found to be destitute, irrespective of whether the child was an orphan or not, and its main focus was on the government's duty to rehabilitate street children by putting them in institutions. The Act covered both neglected or homeless children as well as those who were delinquent, and this unusual association of street children with delinquency has remained central to Indian legislation and official practice since that time.

Fourteen years later, in 1974, a national policy on children was formulated. This was in part a belated recognition that India was a signatory to the 1959 UNICEF convention on the Rights of the Child, and its emphasis was on children's welfare. The policy included the requirement that 'special assistance' should be provided to children from the so-called 'weaker sections', meaning children from lower castes and tribes. This is probably of little relevance to street and railway children, since there is little distinction between them in terms of caste or tribe when they are on the street or the platform, or when they have been institutionalised.

The Juvenile Justice (Care and Protection) Act, 2000 was originally drafted in 1986 and was further amended in 2002 and 2006 in order to ensure that it was compliant with the United Nations Convention. This Act covers street and railway children under the heading of 'children in need of care and protection'.

The Act states how these children should be rehabilitated. The first option is to reintegrate them with their families, followed by sending them to children's institutions and shelter homes. The Act states that the primary aim should be to return children to their families, which is of course consistent with what Sathi does. It also emphasises the role of NGOs in the care of street children.

The Act also covers juvenile delinquents, who are generally described using the more politically correct phrase of 'children in conflict with law', and it stresses the need to protect and rehabilitate children who have broken the law. This Act is generally considered to be very progressive, and it has been further strengthened by the addition of 'Model Rules' in 2007. Remarkably, children under the age of 18 are not allowed to be detained in prison. This is a much more liberal regulation than that which applies in many so-called 'developed' countries, such as the UK, although, like many such regulations, it tends to be honoured more in the breach than the observance.

Institutions for Children in Need of Care

The Government of India works through the mechanisms of the different states, and the level of provision tends to be inadequate in quantity and in quality. The Juvenile Justice system in India covers both children who are in conflict with law and those in need of care and protection, The Juvenile Justice Act (JJ Act, 2006) provides for four types of homes for children and juveniles. They are:

1. Observation Homes (Section 8)
2. Special Homes (Section 9)
3. Children's Homes (Section 34)
4. Shelter Homes (Section 37)

While observation and special homes handle juveniles in conflict with law, children and shelter homes deal with children in need of care and protection.

These homes and institutions come under the purview of the Ministry of Women and Child Development (MWCD) in each state. There are at least institutions for each district in most states—homes for boys and homes for girls in need of care and protection, homes for boys in conflict with law, rescue homes for abandoned women and orphanages for infants. In practice, the capacity in such homes bears little relation to the actual requirements in a district. Much larger facilities are required in major cities and large towns while the facilities in smaller places are not fully utilised.

For example in 2011–2012 Maharashtra State had 32 Children cum Observation Homes, 2 Observations cum Special Homes and 1 After Care Home run by the Govt and supported NGOs for 49 Children cum Observation Homes, 2 Special Homes and 6 Aftercare Homes (ICPS 2012) (Minutes of 42nd PAB Meeting, June 2012).

Apart from the government children's homes, there are large numbers of children's homes or institutions catering for the short and long term needs of children who are alleged to have broken the law and for those who are 'neglected or homeless' or 'in need of care and protection'. Many of these are run by voluntary agencies, supported by donations from within India or abroad, and in some states there is close and effective collaboration between the state government and the agency. In many cases, such homes are also used as hostels for children who have not run away from home, but whose parents want their children to attend schools which are too far away from their homes to come and go every day. These are, in theory, registered and regulated by state authorities, and children may be placed with them, but the standards of these homes vary widely. Some are well-run, humane and homely; others are more like warehouses for children.

Sathi, as we shall see, deliberately works very closely with government children's homes and with other official institutions. Unlike many activists and NGOs whose managements take the view that the government system is beyond reform, and that they must themselves perform tasks such as taking care of children's welfare, Sathi believes that government should and will be the major provider of services of this kind. Sathi sees its own role as a pioneer, a catalyst, a collaborator and a supporter of the government, rather than its replacement or critic.

Regulatory and Supervisory Arrangements— Child Welfare Committees (CWCs)

The Juvenile Justice Act (JJ Act) stipulates that a Juvenile Justice Board (JJB) and a Child Welfare Committee (CWC) should be set up in each district as quasi-judicial bodies with the representation of civil society. The JJB consists of a magistrate and two social workers, of whom one must be a woman, and its task is to deal with children who have been in conflict with law. Chapter III of this Act deals with children in need of care and protection. Section 29 (1) of the JJ Act provides for constituting one or more CWCs in each district to deal with their needs. According to section 29 (2) of the JJ Act, the CWCs shall consist of a chairperson and four other members. One of the members 'shall be a woman and another, an expert on matters concerning children' [Section 29 (2)].

The responsibilities of the CWCs relate closely to the children with whose welfare Sathi is concerned. They are intended to protect abandoned children, orphans, child labourers and runaways, and children who are victims of physical and sexual abuse. Any child found 'in need of care and protection' must, in theory, be produced before the CWC by the person who finds the child within 24 hours. In terms of Section 2(d) of the Juvenile Justice (Care & Protection) Amendment Act, 2006, CWC orders that the child should be conselled. It issues orders to trace the parents or relatives of the child within a week. If parents are found within the district, they are called for counselling. Before restoring the child, the CWC asks for a home enquiry of the family to find out whether the family is fit to care for the child. The committee is empowered to order re-integration of the child with the family, if it is deemed to be in the best interest of the child.

A CWC identifies fit institutions for providing care to such children in the district and visits them for physical verification and recommends such institutions for approval by the state government. It continues to visit the approved institutions and suggests necessary actions to improve the children's situation. It usually reviews the individual care plan of each child who lives in the home. It gives valid suggestions to improve the quality of care. It can direct an officer-in-charge of a children's home to submit a quarterly progress report of any child, and meet the child for an annual review of the progress. If the child belongs to another district or another state, he is sent there with the findings and recommendations of the CWC. It deals very firmly with those who abuse children, and can order filing of police cases where needed. These tasks get modified to suit local needs.

Child Welfare Committees in Practice

The CWC is a relatively new phenomenon and the members themselves are gradually discovering its full potential. Organisations such as Sathi have been quick to recognise the opportunities that this system offers for civil society to gain entry into the government's institutions for children. The actual performance of the CWC system varies widely across the country. In the states where it has been working well—such as in Maharashtra, Karnataka and New Delhi—the committees take effective measures to improve the working of government homes.

The 2005 study in eight cities in northern India found that CWCs had not yet been set up in many districts. Further, many of the senior police and railway authorities had never heard of them. By 2010, 548 Child Welfare Committees had been set up, some of which covered more than one district, so that the coverage of India's total of 640 districts was nominally more or less achieved. Sathi has been eager to work with and strengthen the CWCs in order to make the best use of the importance they give to family reunion. The research studies supported by Sathi have been very useful in highlighting the practical issues and problems of the CWCs themselves as well as the challenges faced by children and their families. For example, the study of 19 CWCs in West Bengal taken up by Shri Mrinal Ghosh, President, CWC, Darjeeling in 2010 sums it up. The CWCs were in place in all the districts by 2008. Their compositions and member profiles matched the stipulations in the JJ Act. They met once or twice a week usually for three hours. Some CWCs handled as many as 900 cases a year while others handled merely 50 cases and the average is around 350 cases. This is more or less the picture in most states. There are still many issues and problems in coordination between the sponsoring government department and the CWCs.

Another contentious area is the CWCs assessment of NGO homes and shelters to certify them to be 'fit' institutions which can be allowed to house children in need of care and protection. If a children's home is not recognised, it is in theory illegal, but many voluntary organisations claim that government recognition

Box 2.1: *Another Take on CWCs*

Geeta Ramaseshan, a Chennai-based lawyer, found her visit to the CWC in January 2012, an eye-opener. It was crowded with impoverished migrants from Bihar, Jharkhand, Chhattisgarh and other states. Their children were taken away on complaints that they are acrobats, beggars or working children. Some were there to claim children caught by the Railway Police. Often, they were unable to prove their identity as parents. Though required to complete an enquiry within four months, the CWC had no means to determine who the parents were in contact counterparts in other states. In this enquiry period the child was entrusted to a reception home in 'protective custody'. Migrant children disliked the food, did not understand the local language and missed their families.

Geetha wonders how the CWC determines that a parent is unfit to keep the child and about the quality of the rehabilitation that the state can offer. She finds that the JJ Act is highly interventionist in its structure. In her view, this goes unnoticed because it is used on the impoverished, who have no access to justice and, therefore, its application is invisible.

Source: Ramaseshan (2012).

imposes lengthy bureaucratic procedures and regulations which are detrimental to the running of the homes, and it is also said that in some states such homes which are perceived to be well-funded from foreign sources have to pay unofficial inducements to secure recognition. The CWCs, on the other hand, claim that voluntary organisations are 'stubborn' and are unwilling to fit into the overall structure which is envisaged under the 2000 Act. Our research and personal interviews indicate that there is insufficient sharing of information between the various parties, in spite of the fact that they are all aiming to achieve the same objectives, and homeless children suffer as a result.

There are additional options in many other countries, such as adoption and fostering, which find mention in the Act. Children in foster care are officially entrusted to a family, or even to an individual, who is responsible for their care, but under the close and regular supervision of the local government authority which placed them and usually on a temporary basis. The foster parents receive an allowance to cover the cost of maintaining the child, or children, as well as some remuneration to cover the cost of their time. There are a number of for-profit agencies to which the authorities out-source the identification and supervision of the foster parents. Some foster parents may eventually adopt the child, if returning home is not an option, but fostering is usually a short to medium term arrangement, pending return home, or adoption by another family. Fostering may last well over the three months 'search time' that is allowed for in the Indian Act. There is a very limited amount of fostering in India, much of which is organised by adoption agencies as a preparation for adoption. This is expected to change in the coming years and the CWCs will have a role in determining which are homes fit for foster care in a district or town. They will be involved in supervising them also.

The CWCs are 'quasi-judicial bodies'; their decisions as to how the children who are brought to them are to be dealt with are legally binding. There is some competition for membership, because of its perceived status and authority rather than any remuneration, or any opportunities for 'rent-seeking'. CWCs are clearly very powerful, since they are effectively the ultimate arbiters of the fate of children who for whatever reason are separated from their families, except in such cases where the children may have broken the law. We found in our research that in view of the variety, urgency and complexity of cases pertaining to abandoned infants or victims of trafficking, runaway boys like those Sathi presents before the committee come low in their priority.

The National Commission for Protection of Child Rights (NCPCR)

In 2007, the Government of India set up the National Commission for Protection of Child Rights, (NCPCR) in order to build national awareness of children's rights. According to the official website, it has to monitor Government's performance and compliance with the 2000 Act, the policy, legal framework and practice, and when necessary to make recommendations for improvements, and to summon violators of children's rights.

This Commission is still in some sense searching for a role. It is trying to encourage a second tier of committees at the town or village cluster level to back up the work of the CWCs. Such an initiative would undoubtedly be very useful, since a typical district in India has a population of well over 1,000,000 people, with some having more than 5,000,000. Allocations are being made for this step in the forthcoming five-year plan.

The Commission is also wrestling with the problem of how to deal with the vast numbers and varieties of Child Welfare Institutions and Residential Children's Homes which already exist. Many are not financed or managed by government, and there is some confusion between the need to introduce a system of 'registration' of such institutions, which would be little more than a list with some minimal formal requirements, and 'certification', which would involve regular inspection and maintenance of standards.

On the issue of children on railway platforms the commission has circulated draft guidelines (yet to be implemented) to improve safety and protection of children on platforms. This approach acknowledges the reality that there are children on platforms who cannot be shifted off it. It identifies the need for establishing linkages between the JJ Act, the Railway Act and the Railway Protection Force (RPF) Act in the best interest of the child. In its view, the railways should take the responsibility to coordinate efforts for child protection in major railway stations. It recommends the formation of a Child Protection Committee with representatives of Divisional Railway Manager (DRM), Government Railway Police (GRP), Railway Protection Force (RPF), Railway Employees (Station Master, Travelling Ticket Examiner, Coolies, etc.), vendors and volunteer organisations who work on child protection issues at or around the railway stations. A CWC near each major station and a Special Juvenile Police Unit (SJPU) by the GRP are also recommended. In addition, they recommend child assistance booths, mid-day meals and short-stay shelters and similar amenities for children living on the platforms.

The document makes no direct or indirect reference to reuniting lost or runaway children with their families or address tracing support to lost children. It is silent about the inherent risks of platform life or the possibility of guiding children off the platform to safer settings either in families or institutions. This is quite a different approach from Sathi's recognition that the number of new children arriving on the platform per day is nearly equal to the resident populations and its strategy of getting children back home from the platform as quickly as possible.

How These Good Intentions Add Up

The law and regulations can be criticised in two respects. First and most obviously because they are incompletely and improperly implemented, and second because there are some fundamental and inherent weaknesses in their design and structure. The Juvenile Justice Act as amended in 2006 is a great improvement on the original Act of 1986, but one major weakness is that its focus has remained on institutionalisation as the main means to rehabilitate children. Harsh Mander attacks the basic logic of sending a vulnerable child to an institution.

> It is absurd and heartless for children to be locked up only because they have no one to protect them. It is argued that this is done for the sake of the child: if the child was free in the community, the State would be unable to protect the child from abuse, and therefore he/she is locked up for his/her own good. This is as illogical as saying that when a woman is gang-raped, and the State is unable to arrest her tormenter, instead they lock her up for her own safety. (Puri, 2009)

Children's rights are necessarily more relative and nuanced than those of adults. Children are and should be regularly deprived of their liberty by their parents, their teachers and others who prevent them from leaving their classrooms or their homes in ways that may injure them. Nevertheless, 'closed' institutions limit their right to live freely, and it is important not to allow the need for protection and rehabilitation to be confused with the notion of imprisonment as a form of punishment. This is particularly important when delinquency and neglect are both covered under the same juvenile justice system.

If a child is officially judged to be in need of care and protection, the law requires that the child should be placed in an approved children's home. Even if such a home is perfect, most children will at first dislike it and may try to escape, as they have already escaped from their family homes. The average age of entry to children's homes is just over 11 years, and the official age of 'graduation' is 18. As time passes, a child may get used to this form of incarceration, but seven years, even of excellent care—in what is essentially a caged environment—is unlikely to enable a child who has grown up in such a place to move successfully into the outside world at the age of 18. The vocational training which is provided in many such homes may enable some children to earn a living outside, but the critical issue is not whether they can earn money but whether they have the necessary skill-set to survive in the world outside the institution.

In addition to its insufficient emphasis on returning children to their parental homes, the 2006 Juvenile Justice Act suffers from a second flaw, in that it does not clarify the role of the numerous voluntary organisations which work in this field. The Act recognises that it is necessary to coordinate the activities of the government and NGOs, and states: 'The State Government may make rules to ensure effective linkages between various governmental, non-governmental, corporate and other community agencies for facilitating the rehabilitation and social reintegration of the child.' But the scope of this provision and the action required to be taken under it are not specified. No details are given of the nature or extent of co-ordination between government and voluntary organisations, and the relationship between them remains haphazard and ambiguous. There are of course many links between the two 'sides'. State governments give financial assistance to children's homes which are run by recognised NGOs, but not all institutions are officially recognised and the official criteria for such recognition are unclear.

There are of course many arguments in favour of the Act and its provisions. Ms Mamta Sahai, for instance, who chairs the CWC in Mayur Vihar in East Delhi, argues that the Act does not promote institutionalisation, because it is clearly stated in the Act that the Committee should endeavour for three months to restore every child to its family, and only after that time should a child be sent to a long-term institution. If a child cannot return home, some sort of disciplined regime is necessary, and if such children are not put in a home, they will soon be back on the street or the railway platform.

There are many cases of effective collaboration. Orissa is India's poorest state and is not known for its effective governance. But in Khurda District of Orissa, for example, the CWC sits in the offices of Ruchika, a large local voluntary organisation which operates a number of informal schools for slum children and also has a small short-term children's home in the same building. The district office of Childline, the national toll-free emergency helpline for children in need, is also based there, and all three institutions work closely together.

Sathi itself, as we shall see later, has also gone a long way in collaborating with the government. It has run several camps actually inside government children's homes, for resident children. This has involved substantial adjustments both by Sathi and by the management of government homes. Sathi had to run the camps in a less open environment, which is much less conducive to self-reflection. The officials of the homes had to accept an alien presence in their midst, designed to get some of 'their' children out of the home and back to their families. This very effective collaboration shows that the barriers between the voluntary and the official mindset are not as impermeable as it might seem.

Challenges Ahead

In general, an appropriate legal and institutional framework appears to be in place to deal effectively with the massive human problem of railway children. Institutions such as Sathi can and do work in close collaboration with the authorities, including the police, and with other voluntary organisations. Laws and institutions can only play a small part in addressing a problem which goes so close to the heart of society and the family, but in the final analysis everything depends on individual parents and on their children. While governments make, amend and execute policies towards protection of child rights and child welfare, families are responsible for providing the right kind of environment to nurture a child. As the United Nations Convention on the Rights of the Child so correctly puts it:

> The child, for the full and harmonious development of his or her personality, should grow up in a family environment, in an atmosphere of happiness, love and understanding. The child should be fully prepared to live an individual life in society...in the spirit of peace, dignity, tolerance, freedom, equality and solidarity. (UNCRC, 2013)

As we were writing this chapter there was heart-rending media reports about two very different situations pertaining to the child in its family.

One was about two young children aged about four and one of Indian Origin in Norway who were taken into care, separated from their biological parents and placed in foster care because the child care system observed that the older child needed specialised care and that parents, especially the mother, was not in an emotionally fit state to offer the required care for the children. The parents were able to mobilise public opinion and get the support of the Indian Government and much media sympathy about such intrusive methods of the Norwegian state. There was much indignation about insensitivity to cultural variations and so on. Given the norms about privacy on such issues the real trigger for this action by the Norwegian authorities will never be known. To complicate matters further, the parents are heading for a divorce and the foster care arrangements seem shaky. The future is still unclear.

Almost in parallel was the tragic story of a two-year old girl 'Baby Falak' a victim of almost savage battering. Baby Falak died after 50 days of battling for life in a major hospital in New Delhi. She was brought to the hospital by a minor girl who actually inflicted injuries on the child. The girl herself was obviously not the mother and the CWC which began to unravel the case found many layers of intrigue. The teenager was first a victim of abuse in her own home, and further abuse in the hands of traffickers. She was then cheated by a man who seduced her and left her alone with the baby he got from another contact. This led to the next layer of truth—the baby had been abandoned, along with her slightly older brother and sister, by their 22-year old mother from Bihar who had, in turn, been sold into a marriage to a man in Rajasthan and had left her three children with the agents who had arranged this 'marriage', trusting them to care for the children. It is evident that there are networks in New Delhi which routinely source children for adoption rackets and the sex trade. Surely there are many children like Baby Falak, her traumatised teen-aged care-giver and women like her mother who are in need of protection and are least likely to appear before the committees set up by the system to help them.

Reporters and analysts who decried the intrusiveness of the Norwegian State were left hoping for the day when the Indian child protection system will develop enough muscle and teeth to prevent such gross neglect and rampant cruelty to children. The system which has emerged in the last few years needs urgent strengthening and rapid scaling up to protect such children in India.

References

Sources

Ramaseshan, Geetha. 2012. 'Norway, yes, but let's also look within', The Hindu, www.thehindu.com/todays-paper/tp-opinion/article2835835.ece; Chennai accessed on 27-09-2013.

Puri, Eshaan. 2009. 'Off the Streets of Delhi: Justice for the City's Children' Working Paper No 233. Centre for Civil Society, New Delhi 2009, retrieved from http://www.ccsindia.org/ccsindia/downloads/intern-papers-09/street-children-233.pdf, accessed on 27-07-2013.

Convention on the Rights of the Child (UNCRC). 2013. retrieved from http://www. ohchr.org/en/professionalinterest/pages/crc.aspx, accessed on July 29-07-2013.

Wikipedia. 2013. 'Constitution of India', retrieved from http://en.wikisource.org/wiki/ Constitution_of_India/Part_IV#Article_39_.7BCertain_principles_of_policy_to_ be_followed_by_the_State.7D, accessed on 3rd August 2013.

National Commission for Protection of Child Rights. 2013. retrieved from http:// ncpcr.gov.in, New Delhi website accessed on 27-07-2013.

Minutes of 42nd PAB Meeting, June 2012, Maharashtra, http://wcd.nic.in/icpsmon/ pdf/PAB-Minutes/mrdtd25072012.pdf, Mumbai, accessed on 28-07-2013.

Chapter Three

Platform Presence

New Arrivals

It was a little past 10 in the morning. Vimla was shepherding three bewildered little boys with ease. She kept up some small talk, apparently about irrelevant things, but carefully noted any personal details that the boys offered inadvertently. She had noticed around six boys who landed on the platform that particular morning. She managed to strike a chord with these three but in the process the other three slipped away. Perhaps they were 'repeat' cases who had run away many times and carefully avoided anyone who seemed too interested in them. It was hot for a morning in October and she was glad that the shelter was very near the station.

One boy, Rahul, seemed very frightened and managed to keep back his tears only because the other two seemed brave. He meekly agreed to go with Vimla because he had simply no idea what to do. He did not join the conversation but held Vimla's hand tightly. The other two boys were more talkative—one of them Vishnu, was boasting about his skills in cricket and the other boy Mihir was reeling off the first names of famous cricketers in India. Vimla promised them that they could play games in the evening when they came to the shelter. Sivakumar Sir would guide them and there were often many matches that they could watch on television. Vishnu nodded wisely. He knew there were many shelters and access to television was a point in favour of this shelter. He was a veteran who had run away thrice from home. He was sure that if things were not okay he could break out.

Mihir kept silent and was happy that he had found a resourceful friend like Vishnu. They would manage to gain their freedom if the shelter proved too stifling.

Vimla stopped at the Railway Police Force (RPF) station near the station master's room. She diligently made entries in the Daily Diary about the children she was taking with her. She quickly completed the First Information Format and obtained the seal and signature of the officer on duty. She requested the constables to keep a watch out for the three other boys she had seen, before they slipped away. They promised to help. She also updated her availability in the movement register kept in the police station. When she began doing platform work, she was a little uncomfortable going to the police station; she also thought the children may get scared. She soon realised that this step was very important—families searching for their children invariably reached the police. Also when the team members had any trouble with either the children or the general public, the police were there to support them.

As she was leaving, she met her colleague Sivakumar. He was coming to the station to plan the details of the networking day Sathi organised regularly on the platform. He smiled at the boys and promised to meet them at the shelter around lunch time. She looked forward to each networking meeting because it was very useful. The policemen, the vendors and luggage handlers in the station were happy to attend and learn about the Sathi team's efforts during the month. The Sathi team also took care to formally appreciate and recognise the help they got from these people who were platform regulars. Sometimes there were parents who came to thank them for their help. She quickened her gait when she realised it was nearly 10:30 am. The children were probably hungry and needed their breakfast.

The shelter was cool and welcoming. It was located in a crowded neighbourhood adjoining a high wall along the railway track. It was a two-bedroom apartment on the first floor. The bathrooms and toilet were set at the back and water was stored in large plastic drums in case the taps ran dry. Vimla introduced the children to the day-time caretaker Gangamma, who took charge of the new arrivals, showed them around and handed out some spare clothes to each of them. Rahul found his a good fit and Mihir's T-shirt hung a bit loose. Gangamma offered hot *upma* and ripe bananas as soon they emerged scrubbed and clean. The boys certainly felt much better after breakfast.

Vimla introduced the new arrivals to the other boys, who were reading or writing something. As they slowly made friends with each other, Vimla noticed that Rahul quickly latched on to Santosh, a boy who had arrived three days ago. Santosh had been travelling with his family and they had to change trains midway. However, he had been distracted by all the things happening on the platform and dragged his feet and it was too late when he realised that he was on a wrong train, which was already moving off. He was found by Sivakumar. Fortunately, Santosh could give his address and contact details and his family was overjoyed to know he was safe. They were expected in the afternoon and he was indeed happy. Life would be good if all their cases were so simple! Her guess was that Rahul too longed to return to his family.

Mihir and Vishnu were happily chatting with two other boys Michael and Shyam—all four were great fans of the Bollywood star Sharukh Khan and were swapping notes on the movies they had seen. Vimla guessed that these were boys who had run away in search of adventure and freedom.

As she looked around, she noticed that two others, Jameel and Vikram, were staying aloof from the rest. They both looked sad and she wondered what story would emerge when then counsellor managed to reach out to them. In her experience, the sullen expression usually meant that the exit from home had been painful—some elder beating or scolding the child or just the fear that some failure would bring on a severe scolding or even a thrashing. Sometimes it was a failed exam or some small sum of money lost or misspent. There was a lot of pent up anger and sadness. Such boys took a little time to relax and share the truth about their lives. Some of them vanished when the staff and counsellors persisted in nudging them to share personal stories. There were no easy solutions in these cases. Each was unique.

Vimla lives in a small town in south India and works for Sathi. She had grown up in a village nearby and completed her high school. She had no clear notion of the kind of job she would find. She only knew that she needed to work. Her uncle, who ran a shop on the railway platform, told her about this NGO and she found the work very interesting and challenging from the very first day. Many trains crossed this junction and Vimla was usually on the platform from 7 a.m. to 10 a.m., looking for 'new arrivals' during peak traffic time. It is tough work—often hard on the back and the legs. She herself came from a loving family and she instinctively extended warmth and affection to these boys. It continued to surprise her that so many of them had run away.

She and her team members were specially trained for platform work and reuniting children with their families whenever possible. She felt very happy when she saw parents meeting their children. Today, there are approximately a 100 young people like Vimla in 18 major railway stations across India working for Sathi. Their work is quite streamlined and the good practices they have evolved and adapted make sure that at least for a few days in a month, all children landing on a platform are noticed and reached out to. Such coordinated action alerts all stakeholders present on the platform and they in turn act as Sathi's ambassadors. These practices are critical for ensuring that children are contacted at the earliest possible opportunity. Therefore they are presented in some detail in this chapter.

Perils of Platform Life

Studies report that roughly 80 per cent of children on platforms are working and 20 per cent are idlers. They are forced to rise early and most of them manage to bathe three times a week. Most of them manage to eat twice a day. They do not have a specified place where they can rest or keep their belongings, if any. They identify a few places which are not too visible and away from the gaze of policemen. Unused drainage pipes, bridges, staircases, trees or the platforms not regularly used serve as their 'space'. Even in locations where NGOs run shelters, only a few avail of them. Children live in groups, perhaps with others doing the same type of work; groups sometimes mark their territory and operate as gangs. Nearly half the children use some form or other of drugs, with 'solution' (or the thinner used for whiteners) being most popular. Products like Dendrite, an adhesive used by carpenters and Erazex, a whitener fluid for correcting typing or writing errors are most readily available. They contain toluene, a sweet smelling and intoxicating hydrocarbon which is neurotoxic. Children can also find tobacco, alcohol or any type of intoxicant at the station if they wish. The police bully and harass them regularly while the railway authorities turn a blind eye. Governments' care services and NGO efforts reach a very small fraction of the whole population of children on platforms.

Some studies have established rampant early-age inappropriate sexual experience among children living for longer durations away from their families on railway platforms. Data from Howrah and Sealdah stations presented by Majumdar is typical of the situation on most railway platforms. Her study reveals that early sexual experience and homosexuality are quite common, especially among the boys. Children who are not even aware of the notion of sexual abuse are the innocent victims. The abusers are usually older platform dwellers or bigger boys more habituated to the platform. Newcomers are forced into such activities and it soon becomes a habit. The children have no knowledge of safe sex or the dangers of HIV/AIDS (Majumdar 2010).

Extended platform stay affects education and long term skill development opportunities of the runaway child, endangers physical and emotional well being, and lures them into delinquency, drug abuse and unsafe sexual behaviour. It is in this context that strategies on the platform have to be understood.

Sathi's Early Interventions in Railway Stations

Early intervention towards preventing a child 'settling down' to platform life is seen as the most appropriate strategy universally.

Over the years, Sathi has refined its practices and regularly uses these on its locations.

A coordinated early intervention effort is organised at least once a month involving all NGOs and stakeholders like the police, volunteers and all available staff. For three days, all platforms of the selected station are patrolled in such manner that most new arrivals are located and persuaded to go to shelters and presented to a CWC immediately. For example, in December 2010, a three-day early intervention programme at New Delhi railway station was organised in collaboration with partner NGOs like Salam Balak Trust and Prayas and 97 children were rescued from the platform. It is estimated that 30 children land on the platforms of New Delhi railway station every day. Thus, early intervention could reach almost all arrivals on those three days. The intensified activity highlights the issue and mobilises all stakeholders into action. Others on the platform like policemen, vendors and porters begin to notice and help children. It also improves coordination among the NGOs and volunteers. This point is further illustrated by Figure 3.1, which reveals that the number of rescues nearly doubles with this approach across locations.

Figure 3.1:
Efficacy of Early Intervention

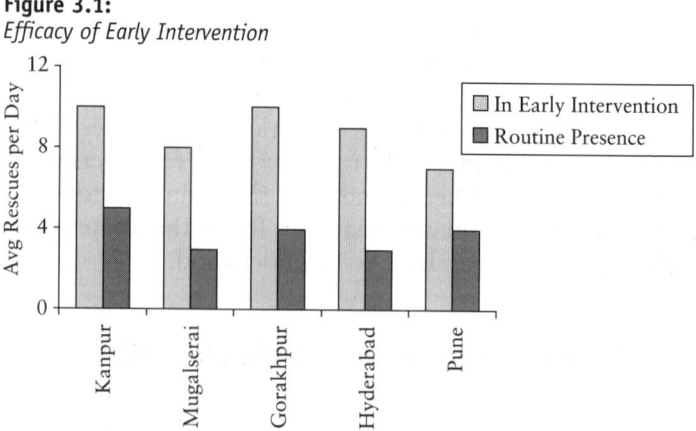

Source: Sathi Annual Report 2009–10.

Networking on the Platform

Sathi organises a networking day in each location. Sathi staff formally visit others actively working on the platforms such as the police, vendors, the maintenance and housekeeping service providers, mobile railway staff like TTEs and canteen staff. They share details of their platform work and seek support. This practice was developed in Bangalore and has been slowly spreading to other areas too.

Sathis's contact point in Kanpur station is a phone booth on platform five. The owner of the booth has begun to look out for children needing protection and guiding them to reach Sathi. He gets to know if they have run away when he catches some snatches of their conversation over the phone. He helped Sathi to rescue 15 children in 2011 (Sathi Annual Report 2012–2013).

Over the four year period of 2009–2013, the police referred 8 per cent of all children brought to shelters and other stakeholders like vendors and coolies brought in 4 per cent of children (consolidated from data in the Sathi annual reports for these four years). The impact of these efforts seems small as of now—yet the details of some these rescues reveal how involved these stakeholders have become.

Sathi observes that after a few years of their intensive work on platforms, the number of children living on the platform

---

Box 3.1: *Vendor Turns Rescuer*

Two girls Pinky and Sankaramma were found on the Pune platform in January 2006. They were not ready to trust the staff. Seeing the situation, Maduri a vendor spoke to the girls and helped the staff to take the girls to safety.

Kiran Kumar, an 11-year-old in Wadi station, stoutly refused to come to the shelter and his resistance attracted the notice of the travelling public. The timely intervention of two constables 'rescued' the staff member from public ire and the boy too was persuaded by the policemen to go to the shelter.

Source: Sathi Annual Report 2005–2006.

has decreased in Bangalore and Pune. As against the 45–50 in Bangalore, the number has declined to four or five and in Pune the number has come down from 70 to around 10 or 12. This is attributed to the combination of early intervention, networking and camps.

However, this is still far short of the requirement. We can understand the magnitude of the challenge of complete coverage, when we consider the fact that only 1,500 children (including the 97 mentioned earlier) were contacted for the whole year in the New Delhi station as against the estimate of 10,800 children arriving on the platforms. In other words, a mere 14 per cent of the new arrivals on the platform were met. The challenge is to know what to do with the children 'rescued' from the potential dangers of platform life. The answer to this emerges from the assumptions or research about why the children have left home in the first place.

Why Children Leave Home

Poverty, dislike of school, problems in the family and the influence of peers are the reasons most often cited by children who decide to run away. NGOs recognise that these children are more spirited than other children in the same situations who are too timid to risk an exit from home. It is this spirit that is celebrated in fiction and film ranging from Dickensian sagas like *Oliver Twist* to more recent efforts like *Salaam Bombay* and *The Slumdog Millionaire*.

Very often, the trigger that pushes a child to leave home is a trivial incident, perhaps the last straw for the child to take. Sathi finds that actual scolding or even fear of a scolding or beating is sufficient to create a panic in the child's mind. Perhaps the boys have had earlier experiences of being scolded and this prompts their action. Many boys leave home in search of work. These boys would not like to go home until they have sufficient money to prove to the family that they have succeeded. Some children run away from the problems they face in the workplace.

Search for adventure or excitement is another factor for running away. Unhappiness in school or hostel is another common reason why children land on the platform. Pressure to complete homework, fear of showing a poor report card, sexual or physical abuse and bullying in hostels are some common reasons.

It is difficult for NGOs and even the government departments to 'solve' these problems. They arise in the child's home context and not on the platform. Organisations like Sathi with their platform presence and shelters have chosen to provide emergency support to the children without going too far into the basic causes. They try their best to help the child and the family to move on and recreate a relationship which is more supportive of the child.

Why Reunification with Family Works

Sathi's follow-up records show that 95 per cent of the children sent back home through early intervention efforts do stay back and settle down to continue either schooling or vocation. The crisis in the child's life has somehow blown over.

Over 90 per cent of the children sent back through camps tend to stay back home, even though their home situation may have difficulties and in spite of them having been exposed to platform life and substance abuse.

Box 3.2: *When Hostel Life Seems Too Tough*

Sathi finds that many children flee from the discipline and strict regimens of residential schools run by religious charities like Mutts and Madrassas. Children report that they are unable to cope with the discipline and feel homesick. They have to tolerate physical and verbal abuse by seniors and at times staff and the parents usually do not pay much heed to their complaints. In the year 2010–11, Sathi rescued 115 children who had run away from hostels run by religious institutions like Mutts and Madrassas. Parents choose these institutions because they give children an education in tune with their religious beliefs at very low cost. They believe they are acting in the best interests of the child's future well being.

Source: Sathi Annual Report 2010–11.

Table 3.1:
Why Children Leave Home

Nature of Factors	Factors	Examples of Reasons for the Child to Run Away
Push Factors	Parent-child relation	• Beatings, scolding at home (for not studying, roaming with friends, stealing money, indiscipline). • Fear of punishment. • Alcoholic parent or close relative. • Stray incidents, petty quarrels at home.
	Challenges at school	• Learning difficulties. • Punishments and shaming in school. • Quarrels with class mates and friends. • Difficulties with paying fees, buying books, etc. • School not well-managed.
	Inadequate parental attention (towards child's concerns)	• Child is interested in studies, but is sent to work. • Child is unable to cope with school curriculum and is either idle at home or sent to work. • Child is forced into a profession without the child's opinion.
	Disturbed family situation	• Divorced parents; single parent. • Child not staying with biological parents. • Family disputes, regular quarrels at home.
Pull factors	Sense of responsibility (on the part of the child)	• Child wants to work to support family. • Child has single parent who is incapable of work due to sickness, disability, etc.
	Unfulfilled emotional needs	• Curiosity to visit a prominent town or city or a place of interest (temple, historic monument). • Impulse (to travel alone on a train, bus, etc.). • Child stays at hostel or with relatives but wishes to regularly meet parents.
Circumstantial factors	External factors	• Natural calamity. • Riots, war or other violence. • Sudden death of parent or sibling.
	Child lost or accidentally separated from parents	• Train/bus journeys. • Crowd. • Large functions (marriages, fairs, etc.).

Source: Nayak 2010.

When children from government institutions like children's homes are sent back to their families, they also stay at home in nearly 80 per cent of the cases.

The experiences of other organisations which are less focused on home placement also indicates that a 'success rate' of 60–70 per cent can be expected.

If children were unhappy enough to run away in the first place and reluctant to return home, this 'sticking' rate is certainly high enough for us to wonder why it works.

The factors which have helped children resume ordinary lives have been identified by Sathi and others too. For example, a 2008 study of 103 children reunited with problematic families revealed that 80 of them stayed back home and 59 reported being happy at home. The study found a significant shift in the behaviour of care-givers towards the child was the single most important factor distinguishing those who stayed on and those who ran away again. Most care-givers reported that they had stopped hitting, scolding or forcing the child and started more explicitly expressing their love for the child. A significantly larger proportion of care givers of retained children reported that they had begun to give more attention to the child and that they noticed improved behaviour in the child and developed a closer relationships with the child (Akhila, 2008). Findings like these repeated across locations over the years have proved to Sathi that they are on the right track in focusing on doing home placement well.

Sathi's Services on the Platform

Everyone agrees that children should be living in homes under the loving care of parents with siblings. Yet, Sathi is perhaps the only organisation which gives it such prominence. Sathi has found it useful to acknowledge that running away is related to the rebellion that goes with the transition from childhood to adulthood. This removes the blame game of finding out who is at fault and goes ahead with improving the situation. Sathi recognises the changing emotional needs of the child on the platform.

The response it has developed takes these emotional shifts into consideration.

When a child leaves home for the first time, there is a lot of anger and hurt. For some it is mere curiosity and adventure. A fresh arrival who has spent two or three days on the platform is innocent and speaks the truth. On seeing the harsh realities of platform life he is eager to get back home. He readily accepts the help and support from Sathi. Sathi realises that the primary need is for reassurance and support which can motivate the child to return.

A child who survives up to a week on the platform has somehow overcome the early fears and doubts. He is trying to settle down into the social system which operates on the platform. He talks to others and seeks their support. He can tell lies effortlessly and is busy swapping tales of adventure with other platform boys. Sathi team members offer guidance and counselling to these children and try their best to inform them about the dangers and long term disadvantages of life on the railway platform. These children may be described as those settling down to platform life. Sathi works hard to move such children to a shelter and offers them counselling and life-skills education.

The third category is the children who are the platform veterans. They feel comfortable on the platform and ready to experiment dangerously. They value their freedom and push away thoughts of home and family and the possible pain the parents, particularly the mother, may be going through. Very often, they have experimented with drugs, sniffing and alcohol. The Sathi camp is designed to help these children resume normal lives. On the platform, the Sathi team keeps in touch with these children and gently persuades them to come to the camp. There are a few fleeting moments of doubt and despondency that these children experience and Sathi's presence to support them in these moments helps them build some level of trust.

The Sathi team is able to clearly recognise these different categories of children on station platforms and reach out to them in appropriate ways .We shall follow the adventures of Sathi and the boys they rescue in all these stages of Sathi's work in the next few chapters.

References

Majumdar, Srabasti. 2010. 'Probing The Presence of Sexual Experiences with a Focus on Same Sex Behaviour in the Lives of Platform Children', unpublished report submitted to Sathi Bangalore 2010.

Sathi. 2006. Annual Report 2005–2006, Bangalore 2007, p. 4.

Sathi. 2010. Annual Report 2009–2010 Bangalore 2010.

Sathi. 2011. Annual Report 2010–2011, Bangalore 2011.

Nayak, Mandar. 2010. ' Events Related to Runaway Children – Factors Leading to Running Away, Child Interactions and Counselling', unpublished report submitted to Sathi Bangalore 2010.

Akhila. 2008. 'Evaluation of Home Placement Strategy among Children in Difficult Circumstances for the Period 2007–2008', retrieved from http://www.sathiindia. org/research.html, accessed on 04-08-2013.

Chapter Four

At the Shelter

A Safe Transit

Many NGOs have set up different types of shelters for street children. There are open or walk-in shelters in all major cities. There are also more secure or permanent shelters which host children for longer durations. Many offer different educational services—ranging from academic to non-formal to life skills and vocations. A Sathi shelter operates a bit differently. Life in the Sathi shelter revolves around immediate support to the children in transit. Children found alone on the platform who can be persuaded to accompany the outreach staff are brought to the shelter. Sometimes a child living on the platform who is sick or otherwise needs help comes to the shelter. This is not very frequent. One layer of activities is around the care of children passing through—feeding them, offering basic amenities and engaging them through a basic routine that is calming and interesting. Frightened or traumatised children coming in, soon relax in this atmosphere. There is no pressure on them either to study or work and there are usually new playmates. Most importantly, there are adults like Vimla who relate to them lovingly and gently. This is often a new experience for children who come from homes where they were scolded or punished regularly. This is an important factor in helping them to consider returning to the family.

Beneath this layer of work in the shelter is the 'investigative' part of their work. The platform educators and counsellors work to discover the emotional issues the child is grappling with. Simultaneously they try to get details about the child's home—addresses or phone numbers that can help them connect with the family of the child. In simple cases where the child has missed a connecting train or lost his way, the family is contacted either directly or through the local police station. There are situations where boys do not want to share their problems immediately and take their time to open up. Counsellors and Non-Formal Education teachers talk to them and probe gently till they are able to trust them and share the real story and family contact details. Often parents are overjoyed to get news of their lost child. They travel immediately or send an uncle or a cousin to fetch the boy home. The reunion is emotionally charged; the intensity of these moments is an intrinsic reward for the staff doing this challenging work. Other boys in the shelter who witness these scenes are often moved too. They begin to long for a reunion themselves and even those who are very angry with their homes begin to recognise the good points about their families. If a family is not able to travel for some reason the child is escorted home by a team member. There are some children who want to go home but cannot provide adequate information to locate their houses. In these cases the shelter team puts on its detective hat.

Let us continue to follow the story of three boys rescued on the platform by Vimla to get a feel of how the system works.

The Daily Routine

Rahul, Vishnu and Mihir chatted lightly as they got ready. They were all around the same age and were similar in height and build. Over the hot *upma* they briefly shared their stories. Vishnu was the most talkative. He claimed that his father was a rich man and a local political leader. The entire village was afraid of him. His two older brothers were also very strong and all the boys in their street looked up to them. He was proud of his family but did not seem to miss them. There was no word about why he left home. He also had stories about different railway stations. Mumbai was the biggest and he loved chicken *biriyani* and *vada pav*. He claimed that he was not afraid of the police because he knew the leaders of all the platform gangs in Mumbai and Pune railway stations. He was talking steadily and there was no need for either Rahul or Mihir to say much. They learnt that they had to wash and stack their plates and that they were expected to clean up after they ate. Mihir seemed surprised and Vishnu showed them both the way to do it quickly and well. He had been taught this by a *didi* (meaning sister in Hindi), in a shelter in Pune, he said.

It was around 11 o'clock when they emerged into the living area, where they saw Sivakumar, whom they had met at the station. Was he the games sir, they wondered. The other boys were crowding around him showing him something that they had drawn. The new comers hung back a little and he noticed this and smiled at them encouragingly even while dealing with the others. He helped the children put up their drawings on a display board and then asked the children to settle down and meet the newcomers. He told them that he was standing in that day for another teacher who conducts some classes which are about general topics of interest to all of them. These were referred to as the NFE classes.

There were five boys in the shelter already. They sat in a circle and introduced themselves to each other again. Sivakumar suggested that they tell each other something about themselves that others are not likely to know. Santosh spoke first. He was beaming. He was waiting for the arrival of his parents and talked about how he loved sweets like *jalebis* that his mother makes. The parents were expected a little after lunch. Michael spoke next. He said he had come away because his step-father beat him up. He had seen a film where the hero leaves home and decided to do the same thing to teach his mother a lesson. He was now repenting his decision and wanted to see his mother. All of them listened attentively to this unexpected outburst. Shyam spoke next and said that he had come searching for work and wanted to get a job as an electrician. Jameel was a slightly older boy and just said he liked to eat ice-creams. Vikram was the last boy to share and declared that he was a fan of the Telugu film star Chiranjeevi. The new comers then shared their names. Rahul said that he loved his grandmother very much. Vishnu said he wanted to become a film star. Mihir said he wanted to become rich. Sivakumar then told them about Sathi and its work.

Rahul was shocked to know that so many boys run away from home. He also realised that the railway platform was not a good place for children. He was a bit surprised at the unrealistic hopes that Vishnu and Mihir had. He was anxious that Vimla and Sivakumar who had been so kind to him would try to find out more about him. He was not sure if he could face his family again after his disgraceful performance in school. He remembered again his mother's hard work and his father's hope that he would study well and get a good job like some other boys in their village.

Vimla joined the group at this point and she told them a story he had never heard before. It was from an ancient Indian epic—the Mahabharata. A little boy, Eklavya, had learnt archery merely by watching a great teacher; but the teacher was not happy with him. All the boys sympathised with the boy and disliked the teacher. Even Jameel took an active part in the discussion about the story which went on till lunch time.

At one o'clock, Gangamma called them to the next room and they were served a hot meal of rice, *dal*, spinach and vegetables. Just as they were finishing, Santosh's parents arrived. They came with fruits and *jalebis* for all the boys. They were extremely happy to meet their lost boy and thanked Sivakumar profusely. Santosh solemnly assured his parents and Sivakumar that he would be more careful and make sure he was safe. The staff recorded the address and contact details and identity proof and gave Santosh some post cards with the Sathi address. Santosh assured them that he would write on the post cards at least once a month and promised to work hard in school too. The happy family left soon because they had a train to catch that would get them home by nightfall. Santosh had been at the shelter for three days but was tearful when leaving because he had become deeply attached to the kind people there and felt very grateful to them.

All the boys watched the emotional reunion, the tears and the laughter and smiles, with rapt attention. Rahul was in tears as he thought of his home. Vishnu who had run away from home twice earlier remained stoic though he too felt a twinge of remorse at the pain his family went through the last two times he ran away. Jameel looked away, unwilling to witness the drama. To lighten the mood, Sivakumar suggested to the others that they could play some indoor games. Vishnu, Mihir, Michael and Shyam were ready to play. Rahul felt sad and said he wanted to rest. Jameel was reading a book. Sunita, the part-time counsellor at the camp, came in during the reunion and she was now with Vikram and they were in another room talking softly. Soon Rahul fell asleep from sheer fatigue.

It was around four o'clock when Sivakumar allowed the boys to go out to play in the yard behind the shelter. They began playing cricket. Rahul was a bit clumsy with the bat and was mostly a fielder. Vishnu was very sure that he could bat very well but got out quickly. Mihir was good bowler and very soon dismissed Vikram who was till then the star batsman in the group. There was a loud quarrel and Sunita the counsellor stepped in and made peace. She was particularly gentle with Vikram though he had been unreasonable. The game continued and the boys soon became friends.

As Sivakumar walked back to the shelter he recalled his early days in Sathi. He had joined the outreach team in a small town. Shelters then were rather like transit rooms. Sometimes children waited in limbo for a month or more till the necessary information was gathered and their return arranged. Over the last few years Sathi streamlined the systems based on earlier experiences. The effort was to send children back home within three to five days in the 'quick turnaround' cases like Santosh's. If they could not find out much within four days of reaching the shelter, the children were taken to the CWC for further guidance or decision-making. Learning from the camp experience, Sivakumar and others in charge of shelters had brought in a routine and orderliness. This gave the boys a sense of being protected and cared for. Also, the activities and routines were such that the staff could observe and understand the child and therefore help him better. There were up at six and were guided through some yoga and some meditative silence till around eight in the morning. After their baths and breakfast they were given some information about Sathi's work and children's issues and rights. This was followed by some life skills and non-formal education and story telling or other creative activities. A rest was mandatory after lunch. They played indoors and then outdoors till dusk. In the evening, the children were encouraged to show their talents—sing, dance, mime and relax. The children's meeting at seven was usually a time when children opened up and shared their deeper emotions. There was talk of people they loved, relationships and memories of good times. Problems in the shelter were also discussed.

Sivakumar also saw the benefit of improved approaches to counselling. The counsellor Sunita was part of an action research project to improve counselling in shelters. He could clearly see the difference now between the child guidance they provided and the deeper level of work that she was engaging in. This definitely motivated children to overcome their fears and to settle down well when they got back home. He hoped that she would make progress with Jameel and Vikram just as she seemed to have helped Michael share his story. At least two boys (Rahul and Michael) had expressed their desire to go home and Harsha, the ace 'detective' of the team, should get on with the job the next day. It was dusk when the boys came in. They were soon sitting in a circle and singing songs. At about seven o'clock Sivakumar came in again and suggested that it was time for the children's meeting. They gathered round him in a circle. Each boy spoke about the thoughts uppermost in his mind. Rahul began by saying that he wanted to return home. However, he was not sure about the location of their village. Sivakumar reassured him and said that they had been able to find out the home with very little data. Jameel was silent till the end. Vikram said that he was sorry about fighting at cricket. Vishnu and Mihir were happy with their day. Dinner was ready at eight and the boys enjoyed the *rotis* and vegetable. They watched some TV and settled down for the night.

Counselling Support

For the boys the next day began early with yoga and silent contemplation. After baths, breakfast and a prayer, the routine was nearly the same.

The counsellor Sunita arrived to talk in detail with the boys who were ready to see her. She first spent time with Michael. He had earlier avoided talking about his home. Knowing that he wanted to talk, she prompted him gently and he shared his feelings of anger and frustration with the situation. Michael loved his mother very much but disliked his step-father. There were many arguments and he knew that his mother was helpless. He wished he could work and earn enough to bring her away with him and take care of her. Sunita worked through this outburst and waited till he calmed down a bit. She asked him if he had thought of what this mother wanted; perhaps she wanted to live peacefully with his step-father and may not want him to work to take care of her. He did well in school and the argument that triggered his exit was about playing truant and watching a film. With Sunita's help he was able to see that his life will be better if concentrated on school. His future will be secure and his mother will be happy if he accepted the changed family context. It took an hour or more to reach this point and Michael gave Sunita his step-father's cell phone number which she passed on to Sivanna.

Talking to Vishnu she discovered that the story of his rich powerful father was made up. She was able to challenge the story gently but firmly. Vishnu began to sulk and said that he will not share any further information. She decided to let him be and and gave him paper and colours to draw what he liked. She was noticing that these drawings usually provided significant clues on what was happening to the child.

She then invited Jameel to spend some time with her. She was intrigued by his drawing the previous day—a picture of a bird in a cage. Did he miss a pet bird? Jameel had revealed nothing about himself since he came. She had taken the picture and kept it with her. She now pulled it out. Jameel looked at it and turned away. He was avoiding Sunita's eyes. She asked him gently if the bird was his pet. He turned sharply and said, 'No, it is me'. She paused and he began talking slowly in a low voice. At first he was hesitant, but soon he was letting out huge sobs and began talking. Jameel had been a student in a regular school till his eighth year. In deference to the wishes of his grandmother he was sent to a residential Madrassa to become a Hazrath (religious leader). He had tried to adjust, but he missed his family badly and when it became too much he just ran away. He talked about his mother, sisters, aunt and father as well as his grandmother. He even missed his pet goat. 'My condition in the Madrassa is like this bird in this cage. I cannot go home and meet my folks. It feels like a jail for me.' He gave his address quite clearly and the phone number. She reassured him that his family will understand his problem and a good solution will be found. He was now gaining confidence that his family could be persuaded to reconsider the whole issue.

It was time for Sunita to wrap up and leave. She felt it had been a very productive morning for her. She knew that Vikram had not indicated any readiness to disclose personal details. She decided to wait and observe him more closely.

Recently she was using more of these experiential tools to relate to children as part of her action research programme in Sathi. She had not imagined it could prove so useful. She had built a repertoire of stories, many of them from biographies of inspiring people across the ages. She found that 20–25 per cent of the children empathised with the story and shared their emotions. This eventually led to trust building and sharing. Another 25 per cent were like Jameel and their pictures revealed their emotions. Sometimes she showed a child pictures and the child described what he associated with it. For example she had shown a picture of a cat snarling at a dog and one boy said it looked like his English teacher. It was obvious that school was the problem for the child. She had a collection of such useful pictures. Sathi counsellors identify children who have been less than a week on the platform and 65 per cent come from this category. Dealing with these children is relatively easy. Twenty-five per cent of the children have been exposed to platform life for more than a week but up to six months. The counsellors try to guide them and many are ready to acknowledge that they are losing out on education and relationships. When the counsellors meet boys who are well into substance abuse and have lived on the platform for more than six months they persuade them to attend a Sathi camp.

Address Tracing

Harsha, one of the staff members at the shelter who was dubbed the 'Sherlock Holmes' of the team, came in and began talking to Rahul. Rahul was able to give the name of his hamlet as Ambedkar colony. This was not of much help because this is a common name for the Dalit localities in many villages. So Harsha continued to quiz the boy by retracing his journey. Rahul was able to provide some further clues. He had got on to the train at a small station about three hours' journey from Hubli, a major junction, where his grandmother lived. He had walked to the station from his village, but did not really know the name of the station. The family usually travelled by bus to visit his grandmother in the large town and he could find his way to her house from the Hubli bus terminus. Since he did not know the name of the railway station where he had started his journey, they could not take a train back. After a little further discussion Harsha and Sivakumar decided that the child would be taken to Hubli bus station. Rahul sounded very certain that he could find his grandmother's house. So that seemed the easiest route to take. It was decided that Vimla would take Rahul to Hubli the next day to locate the grandmother's house as she knew the place quite well.

Harsha was sure that Rahul would indeed locate his grandmother's house. He hoped all would be well and the child safely reunited. He remembered what he had heard at a recent staff retreat.

Sahel, a six-year-old boy was found on the station platform in Kanpur. The child was too young to provide details of his address or family. He was encouraged to draw his house. The staff understood that there was a bridge and a peepal tree near his house. With this information they took the child in a rickshaw to the different bridges in the town. The child identified his house near the Unnao, Kanpur Bridge.

Rahul was older and quite smart too. When the children gathered for their evening meeting, Sivakumar was looking happy.

He had just spoken to Michael's mother, a primary school teacher and his step-father, who worked in a government department. They had been very worried about Michael and his mother had fallen ill. They had spoken to Michael also and promised to come the next day to take him back. They sounded eager to come to the shelter. If he had any doubts after meeting them, he would take Michael's parents to the CWC. Definitely it was a case for close follow-up. Michael, of course, was beaming and he looked ready to sing and dance. The CWC was to meet the next day. Sivakumar decided to present Vishnu, Mihir, Vikram and Shyam and seek permission to keep them in the shelter for a few more days till the tracing of their addresses was completed. Rahul would go to Hubli with Vimla and Michael's parents would come for him. The team would make efforts to contact Jameel's family and start a process of dialogue with them.

The experiences of Rahul, Vishnu and Mihir at the shelter are typically what happen in all Sathi shelters across the country. The outreach team leaders like Sivakumar coordinate and supervise the activities of the outreach team members like Vimla and Harsha. There is a shelter-in-charge, the NFE teacher, the counsellors and a housekeeper/cook in each shelter. The leaders are well-versed in all aspects of Sathi's work and deal with the head office and other offices of Sathi. The team leader also deals with the head office and takes in critical or emergency situations takes quick decisions in the best interests of the child.

The Child and the Family

Regular visitors to the Sathi shelters and camps find that each child has a unique story and a special problem or issue. It is commendable that the staff members are able to catch the nuances of each case and act promptly despite this bewildering complexity. Over the years, Sathi has found that the act of running away arises from the interplay of two major factors—the individual personality of the child and the psycho-social family context.

64   *Rescuing Railway Children*

There may be other concomitant factors like the challenges of education or peer influence at times. An approximate classification of the data gathered over the years has yielded the following pattern and this has proved useful for Sathi in defining its strategy.

It was found again and again that around 31 per cent of the children are moderately well-behaved and come from reasonably caring families. Sixteen per cent of the families are very caring even though the child may have some behavioural issues. Another 16 per cent are from families which are poor or have other problems and the children themselves do not have a major behavioural problem. Children with particularly delinquent behaviour are equally like to be found in any sort of family.

Sathi finds that reuniting with family is highly likely to succeed in these cases which add up to 63 per cent of the children they rescue. Around four per cent are particularly difficult children coming from particularly difficult families and family reunion is not an option at all in these cases. In the remaining cases (33 per cent)

Table 4.1:
Distribution of Children Found according to Family and Personal Traits

Family	Dysfunctional Behaviour	Mild Behavioural Issues	Well-behaved Children	Total Number
Dysfunctional families	3 (3.5%)	5 (6 %)	2 (3%)	10 (12.5%)
Families with moderate problems	3 (3.5%)	14 (18 %)	13 (16%)	30 (37.5%)
Caring families with few problems	2 (3%)	13 (16%)	25 (31%)	40 (50%)
	8 (10%)	32 (40%)	40 (50%)	80 (100%)

Source: Mathani (2009).
Notes: Percentages to the total, i.e., 80 given in brackets. Figures highlighted in grey indicate cases which need adequate preparation before family reunification and close follow-up. Figures highlighted in black indicate need for options other than family reunification. (See also Figure 1.1.)

there has to be adequate preparatory work with the family and the child at the time of reunification for it to work well. In such situations, the child is first persuaded to attend a camp and the long term resolution is worked out thereafter. Sathi's endeavour has been to continuously improve the service offerings for all these children and their families so that children opt to go back home and families make the effort to reach out to their children and keep them home.

Adventures in Detecting Addresses

One service which Sathi has mastered is that of tracing the addresses and locating the families of children from the incomplete and scrappy information they provide. The shelter teams have developed several innovative techniques and we describe a few examples of their ingenuity here.

When a phone number is given by the child, Sathi immediately contacts the number to locate the family. 40 to 50 per cent of the children are able to provide some telephone contact details. The team is continuously surprised at how the children are able to give numbers after many months on the platforms. With the spread of mobile phones, telephone contact has become easier than before.

In the absence of a number, the first clue is the name of the place the child is from. This is not as easy as it sounds. Often there are several places of the same name. A child may name a locality but not be able to name the town or village accurately. There are language barriers and the child's pronunciation or dialect is not easy to follow. In some cases the children were found to be speech and/or hearing impaired.

Sathi relies very heavily on the police force—when there is a rough idea that a child hails from particular place, they obtain the phone number of the police station, using the internet if needed, and call the station directly seeking information on any cases of lost children. The police have helped Sathi to locate the homes in 40 to 50 per cent of the cases over the years. This is of course

Box 4.1: *A Special Case*

Akshay (13) was found by Sathi roaming alone in the Bangalore city station. He did not utter a word in response to the attempts made to talk to him and the Sathi team realised that he was both deaf and dumb. He managed to write the names of his parents and that was all he could do. One team member noticed his school belt which had a buckle with the name of his school in a peri-urban village. Sathi immediately called the police station in that village and spoke to them about their finding the boy. It so happened that the child's parents were sitting in the police station registering an FIR at that very moment! They had searched for the child in many neighbouring towns and were extremely worried about the child's safety particularly because of the challenges he faced with speech and hearing.

Source: Sathi Annual Report 2010–11, p. 75.

Box 4.2: *A Police Official Comes to the Rescue*

Ashbabu (10), was out of home for seven months and Sathi met him. He said that he is from Firozabad. When they contacted the police station, the assistant operator there, Mr C. K. Dixit, flashed wireless alerts across all the police stations without getting any 'missing person' report about a child matching the description of this ten-year-old. Notices in the newspapers were also tried but were of no avail. The staff sat down with the child again and tried to map the direction he gave about the location of his home. He described a circle he would cross outside the railway station at a place called Derabanjara. He would then go past a government hospital and then a bus stand. On the right there was a small flour mill and a beyond that a grocery store. The child gave the name of the store owner and said his home was opposite the store. When this was communicated to Mr Dixit, he confirmed the location as Trilokpur. The parents were then traced and a reunion followed. This trail was established in about a month's time.

Source: Sathi Annual Report 2009–10, p. 79.

contrary to the image of the police as a callous force not sensitive to children's needs.

Besides the police, options successfully used by Sathi for address tracing include the Panchayat office and the Post Office. The police are able to provide these numbers even if they are

Box 4.3: *Sathi's 'World Wide Web'*

On 1 November 2011, Mohammad Sagar alias Majnu was referred by Sathi to Bangalore Government Home. He was rescued from the Bangalore railway platform and was brought to the shelter. The boy seemed like he suffered from speech and hearing impairment. On observation, the staff felt that the child was could speak but was not yet ready to interact.

Many attempts were made to evoke some response. A Sathi counsellor sitting with him showed him many kinds of images from the internet. When they saw a map and images of some places in Bangladesh, the child shouted with joy, *'Yeh Mera Desh Hai!'* ('This is my country!') He had come from Bangladesh and could certainly speak Bangla well. The officers in the government home informed the Railway Police Force at Yeshwanthpur and sought their help to send him to Bangladesh.

It took more effort to draw complete information. Initially the child lied that his parents were staying at Surat in Gujarat. After a week, he said his parents were still in Bangladesh and gave names of his father and uncle. His father was a rickshaw driver and his mother had expired. He had left home five months ago because his step-mother used to beat him. He named his village and district quite clearly though he did not know any phone number. He had entered India through Benapul Gate and had reached West Bengal, from where he had taken a train. He did not have a visa, passport or any other documents. He had wandered around, sweeping and begging to earn his livelihood.

This was immediately reported to the Police Commissioner, Railway Police and local police as an illegal entry. To enable faster repatriation, Sathi decided to transfer the case to New Delhi. A request letter regarding his release was given by Sathi staff to the CWC, Bangalore. He was then taken to New Delhi along with Sathi staff and an RPF staff. The Sathi Programme Officer (who could speak Bangla) informed the Bangladesh High Commission and presented the child to the CWC in New Delhi. The child was sent to Salam Balak Trust.

In the mean while, Sathi in Bangalore continued the efforts to trace his family. Through the internet, his profile and photo were sent to the Bangladesh police. This did not evoke a quick response. The phone number of a health care centre in the district was found on the internet. When Sathi contacted this number and related the story, the staff there rallied round to help. They provided the correct contact number for the Police of Control Room. Details of the child were given to the appropriate police authorities. Regular follow-up for almost fifteen days yielded fruit and the boy's uncle's contact number was traced. Conversation with the family was initially difficult because of language barriers and the Delhi team of Sathi took over. The child's uncle came to Delhi to take the child home from Salam Balak Trust.

not able to investigate the child's family details. Another option works well for Sathi. If there is a family in that place whose child has been reunited by Sathi, they are called over phone and they come forward to help. Google Maps has been a great resource of late.

Public announcements, newspaper pamphlets and local television announcements have all been tried in turn when needed. When all these efforts fail, Sathi escorts the child to the place he mentions or describes and locates the home then restores him to the family. Sometimes this happens even when the child is ambivalent about his return.

Nine-year-old Rakesh was found on Secunderabad railway station and he said that he came from a neighbouring locality called Lalaguda. He was very afraid to go home and gave the locality name after nine days in the shelter. When a staff member took him there, they walked around for an hour and the boy did not indicate where his house is. As they were about to give up and return, a friend of Rakesh came by and talked to him. This boy guided them to the house and the reunion was a happy one on all sides. The staff member realised that the boy know his address and the location of the house well enough and was reluctant to divulge the full particulars.

Incomplete addresses could prove challenging as well.

Sadiq from Delhi was found in Gorakhpur railway station. When the boy realised that Sathi would approach the police, he got scared and gave the name of his employer. After denying any knowledge of the child, the employer acknowledged his action and contacted the child's father. It took Sathi three months to complete the whole cycle.

This intensity of efforts to locate the family is one of the major reasons why Sathi succeeds in achieving this large number of reunions where others have not been able to make headway. The Sathi shelter teams have become experts in tracing addresses and they are able to reunite most of the children despite heavy odds. It is now able to offer address tracing as a distinct service to other institutions like government children's homes.

References

Sathi Annual Report 2005–08. Analysed by Dr Rajshri Mathani of TISS for Sathi.

Mathani, R. 2009. Retrieved from http://www.sathiindia.org/sathi%20doc/Ourwork/Conceptualization.ppt, Bangalore, 2009, accessed on 1 August 2013.

Sathi. 2010. Annual Report 2009–2010, Bangalore 2010, pp. 75, 79.

Chapter Five

Protection for Children in Need

An Outing in the Sathi Van

As he woke up the next morning, Vishnu realised that the two days he had spent at the shelter had been quite exciting. He was a bit disappointed that the lady who had spoken to him had seemed sceptical about what he had said. Women like her were usually very sympathetic in the other shelters. This one seemed a bit tough. Perhaps Sivakumar sir would be kinder. He was a bit thoughtful and reflective as he went about the early morning routine. Soon it was time for the Non-Formal Education class and they expected to meet the actual teacher who was coming back from leave. However, around 10:30 am, Sivakumar came in and asked Vishnu, Mihir, Vikram and Shyam to get ready to go out with him.

The CWC for the district met every Thursday at the government children's home and this was a good 10 kilometres away from the shelter and the railway station. When Sivakumar herded the four boys Vishnu, Mihir, Vikram and Shyam into the Sathi van, it was almost fun. Vishnu was the most carefree as he seemed to know what to expect. The other three looked scared and defiant at the same time. Sivakumar tried to get them to relax. He explained that they were going to meet an auntie and three uncles who are appointed by the government to take care of children who are lost and homeless. Mihir reached out and held Sivakumar's hand and said, 'Will they let me stay in Sathi shelter?' Sivakumar explained that the committee will talk to them and decide. He advised them that they should try to answer all questions put to them truthfully and clearly so that the committee could take a good decision.

The van drove up to the porch of a building set in a pleasant campus set a little away from the bustle of the town with flowers, trees, open space and a playground. This was the only government home in the district, built to accommodate a one hundred children at a time, including 40 girls. Separate sections for infants and for abandoned women were both set in the same complex. The buildings were in a fairly good state of repair and maintenance. Vikram, who had not said much so far looked up at Sivakumar and said, 'Looks okay, doesn't it?' Sivakumar immediately used this comment to reassure them that it was a good safe place, and that Ranga, a Sathi representative, was available on the campus for all the children there every day.

As if on cue, Ranga, who had been waiting inside, stepped out to welcome Sivakumar, on hearing the van. After introductions, he offered the boys some biscuits and tea and settled them down to watch television in the common room. The common room was empty because the children in the home were at school. They walked to a nearby school and went home to their families during holidays. Some of them were in fact admitted there by parents who could not take care of them. There were actually 90 boys in the home and 31 were such admissions. After intensive counselling, Ranga guessed that only 17 boys were actually homeless and in need of care and protection though the others preferred to maintain they did not know their address or that they were orphans. Sathi estimates that 70 per cent of the children in homes are runaways. Homes in big cities like Delhi and Mumbai are more crowded and some district homes are almost empty.

Sivakumar and Ranga discussed the profiles of the four boys and decided to seek permission to keep all four of them in the shelter for a few more days. They were not sure if the CWC would accept this request. Another possibility was to send Vishnu, who was clearly a repeat runaway, to a Sathi camp that was scheduled to start on Monday. Similarly, Shyam and Vikram too could be sent to a camp to really find out what their stories were. Mihir seemed a first time runaway and seemed likely to share his story if persuaded. So they could request for access to him for a few more days. There was a possibility that the CWC could decide to send all the boys to the government children's home. In that case, Ranga would continue to meet them and try to find out their real stories.

The Committee Meets the Children

Ranga got busy preparing the records for the meeting. He assisted the CWC with its paper work, almost performing the role of a secretary. This is one of the ways in which Sathi strengthens the working of CWCs. The meeting was scheduled for noon. It was, as usual, held in a spacious well-lit room at the government children's home. Sivakumar and his wards arrived at about 11:40 am and soon one of the four CWC members arrived. He was 10 minutes early and chatted with Sivakumar, who knew him well as an advocate in the town who was ready to help with cases about children's needs. The other members came in within the next few minutes and somewhat unusually for such occasions, the meeting started more or less on time.

All members were trained lawyers, though three of them now worked in different fields. The chairperson was a lady and a senior social worker, another was involved in public health and the fourth member was semi-retired from his legal firm and teaching Constitutional Law at a nearby college.

Besides the four boys and the carry-over from previous meetings, there was a young woman who sat silently and sadly at the end of the room, waiting for her case to be considered. She had apparently been a victim of a sexual assault and the CWC would hear her in privacy to decide on permission for her to stay in the women's short stay-home also in the same campus. A small and affectionate puppy walked in and out of the room during the meeting, and the atmosphere was generally informal and totally unthreatening, quite unlike what might have been expected for a meeting of a formal body with quasi-judicial powers.

Ranga presented the minutes of the previous meeting. The members talked about some of their earlier and as yet unresolved cases before taking up new ones.

A 12-year-old boy, Amir, had attended a camp which Sathi had organised a few weeks earlier. He had been rejected by his mother and his step-father. She had divorced his drunken and violent father and remarried and now had three younger children with her new husband. The boy had told Sathi's staff at the camp that he wanted to go to live with his grandmother, who would also allow him to see his father. This seemed to be a reasonable solution to Sathi, but one member of the committee had felt that the grandmother was not capable of supporting the child, so the matter had been deferred for further consideration in the last meeting. Ranga shared a report from the local police on the grandmother and her resources which confirmed her capacity to take care of the child. The committee decided to allow the child to go to his grandmother and instructed Sathi to maintain a monthly follow-up for six months. (Authors' personal observation)

Another boy, Karun, was from Nepal. The regulations required that he should be sent back to his native village in Nepal, but this would have to be negotiated through the Nepalese embassy in New Delhi and would take many months. The committee wanted to refer him to their counterpart CWC in Gorakhpur, on the Nepali border, where such cases could easily be arranged with the local border staff, but the official arrangements only allowed children to be referred to committees in their home districts. The child therefore had to remain in this home. Listening to this Sivakumar wondered if it would be possible to send him to a Don Bosco vocational centre in Bangalore and made a mental note to chat privately with the CWC chairperson later. The children were not present during the discussions and the committee decided to meet them and explain the decisions to them after the day's agenda was concluded.

The four new children were then called in together. The chairperson smiled graciously and to their surprise and delight offered them some candies. They were polite and stood meekly till they were asked to sit down. The committee members immediately recognised Vishnu, who had apparently appeared before the committee twice before. They greeted him light-heartedly, and he responded in kind, without being overtly cheeky. He was an orphan, and had been living with his brother, but he enjoyed the freedom of the railway station and seemed to have run away more or less for fun. Sivakumar wondered whether this was true and why Vishnu had not confided all this to them over the two days. Vishnu was told that he would be taken home, that he must not run away again and he promised that he would not. The committee members were not so sure. At this point Sivakumar intervened and suggested that he could be sent to the forthcoming camp where he could get an opportunity to consider what he wanted to do and then return either to his cousin or enter an appropriate educational institution. This was agreed upon because it seemed better than sending him home or keeping him in the children's home. Vishnu continued to be nonchalant and had no particular anxiety about going to the camp. He seemed to know that he could take almost anything in his stride.

Mihir was presented next. He continued to state the same version that he had offered to the shelter counsellor, though she was not sure that was the truth. He was thirteen years old and had run away from an unhappy home situation from a village close to the city. He had stayed for some time on the station railway platform and admitted that he smoked regularly and also sniffed 'solution'. He rather naively asked if these habits were 'all right' and promised to stop when he was told that they were not. The committee decided that he should remain in the children's home for a fifteen-day 'observation' period before a final decision was made as to where he should be sent. Mihir was a little nervous now. He said that he had never been to school, so the committee agreed that he should not have to go to the neighbouring local school with the other inmates of the home, but could remain in the home. He was relieved that he did not have to bother with lessons. He thought it would be fun to just hang around this place and play with the other boys when they came back from school. Perhaps he would be allowed to watch the television which seemed to be the only form of activity which was provided for the children during the weekend or after school. Ranga made a note that he should keep a watchful eye on him and look for a breakthrough. The committee members and the Sathi team thought privately that he looked as if he had been sent to school.

Shyam who went up next shared much more than he did in the shelter. He had worked with his father in a brick kiln. The work was hard and he ran away one day when he was completely fed up. He reached the railway station and found that he could make money easily if he collected bottles. He wandered all over and had seen Mysore and Bangalore and reached this town. On the platform he helped a vendor who fried *vadas*. The police got after him one day because his employer thought he had stolen some money. The police handed him over to Sathi because it turned out that the money was not missing after all. He declared that he had forgotten his home address and wanted to go to another government home. He also admitted that he liked to sniff solution and had missed it during his stay in Sathi. The committee was sure that he was not in conflict with law because he had come to Sathi through the police.

The lady heading the CWC ruffled his hair and asked him gently, 'Which home is better—this home, another home or your family home?'

Shyam replied promptly said, 'Another home'.

She persisted, 'Okay, but if you have to choose between this home and family home?'

He was tired of his wandering and needed to rest somewhere. May be his parents would see him differently now. He hesitated and then replied, 'Family home'. The CWC decided that he would be sent to the camp. Ranga was intrigued by his request to go to 'another home' and made a note to probe this further.

Vikram, who came in next, remained sullen and said he was an orphan and had lived on various railway platforms ever since he could remember. He avoided eye contact and seemed unhappy. The committee tried in vain to know more about him. They decided he should stay in the children's home and the staff there should try to get him to share more details. Ranga too could help when possible. The meeting had gone on for two hours and the committee still needed to talk with the sad young woman sitting at the back of the room.

The Sathi team and the boys took their leave at this point. Sivakumar and Ranga were happy for the moment. The meeting itself was pleasant and informal. Sivakumar had heard during the informal discussions in the Sathi staff retreats that the atmosphere was very different during the CWC meetings in some other places. He felt that if all the hundreds of such committees in India are as unthreatening, the system should on the whole play a positive role in many children's lives. Two children had been sent to the Sathi camp, but might well come up again. A final decision on the other two was to wait until they had been 'observed' for two weeks. In the meanwhile, the shelter had called to say there were three new arrivals. The children were given lunch and Sivakumar left with Vishnu and Shyam. Both of them were a little subdued because two friends had been left behind and also because they were a bit tired with the travel and the waiting. They would have to wait three more days in the shelter before going to the camp. Vishnu had many questions in his mind about the camp. But Sivakumar was silent and he did not want to bother him.

The Children's Home

Ranga took charge of Mihir and Vikram. He asked them to wait in the common room till his CWC work was over and returned after an hour. He then took them to meet the Welfare Officer Ms Chitra, who made the boys sit down. She took her time asking the boys various questions and writing down their answers. She then assigned them to two different dormitories and provided them with two sets of clothes, sheets, pillows, a comb, coconut oil, soap, shampoo and other toiletries along with a bag for personal belongings. They were also provided with some books to read even though they were not expected to join school. Ranga took the boys and introduced them to some others in their respective dormitories. The children were straggling back from school and some were intent on completing their homework before play time. Each boy felt a pang, as they went their separate ways, though Vikram and Mihir had hardly spoken to each other in the Sathi shelter.

There was a buzz of excitement in the home. A national politician who lived in the district had decided to distribute to the children's homes the sweets he received on his completing three years in office. All the boys were summoned to the quadrangle in the middle and they lined up to receive their share of sweets. In general, the rules do not allow food from outside. However, the sweets were all good quality and came from a safe source. Therefore, an exemption was made. The children received sweets and were now ready to play till dusk.

Mihir and Vikram went out to the field along with the rest. They watched the groups settling in. There were three or four groups playing cricket. The youngest ones of around seven years of age were merely running about and there was a group on the football field. There was also a group around a basketball ring on a tree trunk. A few were merely on-lookers. Vikram noticed that Mihir was eager to play and looked at him and nodded, 'Why don't you go join in?' he urged.

Mihir hesitated and wanted Vikram to join in too. However, Vikram preferred to stay out and pushed Mihir to join in. Slowly Mihir edged towards a group playing cricket. The boys were around his build and age and he felt he could fit in there. The captain of the game noticed his approach and gestured him to get into a fielding position. Mihir soon relaxed and felt at ease. He could hold his own at cricket and therefore immediately gained acceptance.

Vikram stayed aloof and was not ready to mix with others so easily. When he went back to his dorm after dinner he stayed quiet. The boy who was the monitor for the dorm smiled at Vikram and offered to help if needed. Vikram smiled back in acknowledgment and soon fell asleep. He woke up suddenly with a start. It was as if some one was tapping under his bed; his dorm was on the first floor. Perhaps a rat; but no...it was definitely a series of taps. He realised that he was in the middle of some nocturnal game and did not want to land into trouble the very first day. He kept his eyes tightly shut tight and waited for more. His dorm leader came up to the bed and peered down at him. Satisfied that he was asleep he whispered to the person knocking and went and opened the door noiselessly. Two figures from the room slipped out into the night. He was worried and could not go back to sleep. Nor did he feel like raising an alarm. It was none of his business and he did not want to be a sneak.

The next morning there was a hue and cry. Four boys from three different dorms had disappeared into the night. All the boys in the three dorms were questioned to no avail. Ranga came in and spoke to the boys. He said that he was very worried for the safety of the boys who ran away. He left a little box and asked them to drop a chit with any details they may have. No one would know who had written it and the boys would be safely brought back. The police were called in. The railway station and bus station were alerted. Vikram overheard a few other boys talking about it in the playground. The runaways were in fact senior boys who wanted to find work and earn to support their families. They had left by the mid-night train to join a friend in a mining town which was one night's travel by that train. That boy had earlier been in the home and had promised them good jobs in a quarry nearby. The authorities continued their efforts to trace the boys and no one shared any of this information with them.

Vikram and Mihir spent a little time chatting when all the school goers had left. Mihir was of the view that there was no point running away to work if all their needs were met. Vikram thought they must be good boys to want to work for their families: but he kept these views to himself. The warden called them at this point and asked them to work in the garden to keep them busy. Vikram worked hard and Mihir did as little as he could get away with. There was a watchful gardener who immediately assessed the nature of the two boys.

When Ranga met them in the afternoon they again discussed the events of the night. Ranga knew the three boys well. He felt bad that he had not known that they were facing a problem. One boy had been rescued from begging and the other two had families in nearby villages. He made Vikram and Mihir solemnly promise that they would stay in the home till a good path was discovered for them.

Sathi in Government Children's Homes

In the evening Ranga left for a review meeting in the Sathi head office about their work in children's homes, rather worried about the two new admissions. Ranga had completed his graduation and joined Sathi. He was willing to do any type of work and eager to learn. So he found himself doing a whole range of jobs within the first year. He started in a shelter with documentation and pitched in for platform work or life-skills classes as needed. Soon he was asked to be in a camp and he learnt the basic camp routine. He often accompanied boys to locate addresses which were not so readily traceable. Therefore, when Sathi gained the opportunity to locate its own staff within government homes, Ranga and others like him who were eager to try all the different types of work were preferred for these assignments.

Fifteen of them were meeting for two days to review six months of work. They had become a well-knit team, sharing and supporting one another across the country. Ranga had some noteworthy developments to share. He was sure that there would be much to learn. They were always discovering new ways to nudge the system to be more sensitive and caring. They also had their share of concerns. They often witnessed behaviour which was rude and harsh to children. Yet, they could not protest openly because they did want continue to work with the children in these homes. They found that in each of the homes the welfare officers were happy to understand their methods and to locate home addresses and reunite children with their families. However, they were ready to give up very easily if a child didn't immediately offer information or gave inadequate information.

Sathi began working within the government children's homes in 2005 to try to reunite the children with their families as far as possible. Gradually, Sathi has improved its coverage and now works in eighteen homes across six states. This team working across the Government Homes had managed to home place over twelve hundred children annually. They initially applied their address tracing skills to demonstrate to the staff how it is possible to find the homes even if there is very little information provided by the child who is willing to go back home. This was possible in 30–40 per cent of the cases. The next stage was to work at a deeper level with those not so willing to return and find out the child's fears and anxieties about going home. Sathi staff took up cases of children staying beyond six months and demonstrated how the combination of counselling and address tracing can be used for good effect.

Sathi's Perspective on Government Children's Homes

Many NGOs have been able to gain access and entry to children's homes across the country especially because the juvenile justice system has created possibilities for interchange with civil society organisations. Most of them work directly with the children providing them education, vocational and life skills. In this process, they have been able to address the emotional needs of the children and help them cope with their lives and the institutions better. The fact that there are visitors who talk with the children has in itself created some measure of restraint and staff members are careful that they are not openly seen abusing or ill-treating children. There are many reports about the lives children lead in these homes and activists are demanding major changes quickly.

Sathi is of course very concerned about the situation. Its response has been to find ways of removing children from this setting and taking them back to their families. Some of the initiatives Sathi has taken in this regard are described here.

Children arrive in the government home after an indefinite length of time away from their families. Most of them declare that they are orphans and the matter is left at that. However, the Juvenile Justice Act mandates that every effort should be made to restore the children to their families within three months. Sathi,

Box 5.1: *Travails of Care and Protection*

As many as 891 children have gone missing from April 2001 to March 2011, from 33 homes located in various districts of the state of Karnataka, according to the official response to a petition filed by Odanadi Seva Samsthe, a social organization working for trafficked women and children. This is an average of 90 children per annum. Moreover, four cases of unnatural deaths of children have also been reported from these homes.

The highest number of children (almost one fourth) went missing from Government Boys Home Bangalore and over 75 per cent of those missing were boys. These figures have raised serious doubts about their safety and security in these homes (DNA 2011).

Many reports of cruelty to children have been authenticated too. For example, in November 2011, Mohammad M. was caned as he did not go for lunch on time. This 14-year-old boy was hospitalized after he was allegedly beaten with a cane by a security guard at the government-run boys' home. A child worker, had been rescued from a bag-making unit by Justice and Care, an NGO. He was waiting to return to his home town Bareilly in Uttar Pradesh. Medical reports stated that the boy had narrowly missed an elbow fracture (Deccan Herald 2012).

The Karnataka State Commission for Protection of Child Rights dealt with the matter. 'Though the boy was beaten ten days ago, the staff there gave him medicines twice a day and hushed up the matter. It would have never come to light, if the people from the NGO had not spotted it', said the chairperson of the Commission. The CWC, which had settled the case, had not been informed about the incident. There were 175 boys in the home and because of staff shortage, the security guard was also taking care of the children. Though no case has been filed against the guard, he has been fired. The Commission said this was not the first case of beating reported at the home (DNA 2011).

based on its good will with CWCs and its track record with railway children, was able to persuade CWCs to try their methods in government homes. Sathi began in its characteristic fashion by talking to children and finding out if some of them wanted to go back home. Many were keen; some of them provided contact details almost immediately. This was a surprise to Sathi staff as well as the staff in these homes. Children simply stated that they had not thought of going home because nobody had suggested this as a possibility. It took five years to build momentum for this work. Sathi's special skills are proven again and again in those cases where the children have been in the home itself for long durations.

Box 5.2: *Tracing The Way Back—With Some Luck*

Take the story of Ajay a twelve-year-old. He was at the government home in Varanasi for over a year. The child was confused and said he could find his home in Sasaramor or Mohania in Dadra District of Bihar. The Sathi counsellor took permission and accompanied the child to Sasaramor. They walked from there to Mohania, stopping to enquire at 60 shops on the way. It was a coincidence that a person visiting this market recognised the child as a boy who was lost from Mohania Kaimur of Dadra. The child could then be reunited with the family and was resettled into school.

Source: Sathi Annual Report 2010–11, p. 76.

Sometimes it is too late to help.

Box 5.3: *A Cold Trail*

Kareemullah, 12 years old, had been in the Hyderabad government home for nearly two years. One day he revealed to the Sathi counsellor that his family lived near the Malakpet railway station with adequate details. On visiting the place, the counsellor discovered that the family had indeed lived there but had moved on. It was not possible to trace their next address.

Source: Sathi Annual Report 2010–11, p. 76.

Sathi soon recognised that some children have to be re-oriented before reuniting with family. There were instances where the address was traced and the child immediately restored to the family from the children's homes and they ran away again. Sathi was able to convince the authorities to send some of the children to camps before attempting family reunions. This was a big step because the authorities were accountable if the child went missing. Again it was the CWC permission that provided them the 'safety net' to send boys out. For Sathi, the risk of the boys escaping from the camps was very real. Thankfully, the first few instances proved helpful for the boys and the home authorities and CWCs had begun trusting the Sathi camp process. This led to a Sathi study of children in fifteen government homes. The analysis which emerged had provided Sathi an understanding of the variation in approach needed in the different cases.

In many cases children were keen to return home and knew their exact addresses. Sathi's intervention is not needed in such cases because the government home staff could very easily restore the child to its family.

There were cases where the child wanted to return but did not have clear details of the address. These were cases for Sathi-style detective work. The Sathi staff could organise physical visits to localities to take up local enquiries, through their own staff, partners, police or other well wishers. This required more time and patience.

There were still other children who resisted the notion of going back to their families and offered clues about their original homes. For such children, the Sathi camp seemed a good answer. Even if the family was not a viable destination, the camps offered the child a space for rethinking and making a choice for a better future.

This analysis was shared widely with the CWCs and the government homes and it has been helpful in determining the cases which need to be taken up by Sathi and the actual type of intervention.

Sathi's work has proved an inspiration to the staff. There is some evidence that this is taking root. From the year 2010–2011 onwards, nearly 1,500 children were restored to their families from Government Homes by their own staff each year. One factor which has convinced the government system is the outcome of the follow-up contacts. Sathi's telephone follow-up over the last four years indicates that 88 per cent of the children stay at home and 43 per cent of them go to school (Table 1.2, chapter 1) and 24 per cent were in some vocation. To strengthen the skills for family reunification within the system, Sathi has organised programmes on counselling skills for the welfare officers and probation officers in these Homes. It has prepared booklets of

20 challenging cases handled in each of the four major government homes (Bangalore, Kanpur, New Delhi and Hyderabad) to circulate to the staff in these homes. This has been found very useful too.

The next big shift was to enrol children from these homes in Sathi's camps for children (especially those with behavioural or substance abuse problems). Issues of procedure and red tape had to be sorted out to actually take children out. This was possible because the CWC could give this permission at a disaggregated level, one of the opportunities arising from the implementation of the improved JJ system. Sathi could settle the children who came to the camp either with their families or in some educational or vocational training institutions. The outcomes were so clearly positive that Sathi managed to hold six camps within the premises of these government homes in 2011. The government staff were able to see what it really takes in terms of effort and dedication to actually guide these children and stabilise them on the path of better integration with society and family. Sathi staff had to adjust themselves to offering a camp within the government rules and limits. The camps were as effective in this setting as anywhere else.

Sathi counsellors like Ranga, working in government homes, are hopeful that many more such camps can be organised within these homes in the next six months. Sathi team members are also very happy that they have been able to work with girls in government homes and restore them to their families. They can at last reach out to the large number of girls in these government homes and go beyond working only with runaway boys. Sathi has been able to gradually transpose the methods used in railway stations into these homes, adapting and refining them as needed. The effort to communicate with these homes across the country has been a stimulus for better documentation and information sharing also.

References

DNA. 2011. 'Children Go Missing from State Run Juvenile Homes in Karnataka', retrieved from http://www.dnaindia.com/bangalore/1531734/

report-children-go-missing-from-state-run-juvenile-homes-in-karnataka, Bangalore, accessed on 29-07-2013.

Deccan Herald. 2012. 'Boy In Governemnt Run Home Thrashed By Guard, Hospitalised', retrieved from http://www.deccanherald.com/content/208270/boy-government-run-home-thrashed.html, Bangalore, accessed on 29-07-2013.

Sathi. 2010. Annual Report 2009–2010, Bangalore 2010.

DNA. 2011. http://www.dnaindia.com/bangalore/report_childrengo-missing-from-state-run-juvenile-homes-in-karnataka_1531734

Chapter Six

A Re-Integration Camp*

The Beginning

Vishnu and Shyam found themselves rolling along towards the camp location by 8 am on Monday. They had been discussing the camp with each other. It had seemed like a picnic when the shelter counsellor Sunita had tried to encourage them to go. But the mood in the bus was gloomy—it was as if they were all being taken to a punishment location. There were nine boys from the government children's home who seemed happy to escape its walls. Four boys had trickled into the shelter in the course of the previous day. Vishnu was surprised to learn that they were being sent to the camp by their parents. The boys were trying very hard to appear nonchalant. There were eight others coming from different NGOs or the railway platform itself. They seemed to be tough guys used to managing on their own. Besides the four camp facilitators there were 21 other boys in the bus. They would be together for a month.

The camp facility was a good distance from town. They got off the main road after an hour's drive. After that, it was a winding dirt track with many smaller roads branching off to villages and habitations. Their camp location was indeed in the middle of nowhere. They reached by about 11 am. Vishnu quickly realised that if he had to run away from here he would have to walk at least a couple of hours—not much to his taste! Some of the older boys also noticed that there were no cigarette or *paan*

---

*Details about boys in this chapter were obtained through observation of a camp and interviews with children, their parents and camp staff. These are presented in italics. For cases selected from Sathi annual reports, references are provided.

shops (selling betel leaf and areca nut combination for chewing, common across India) in the neighbourhood. They were a bit surprised that the camp teachers were so young and didn't seem tough at all. As the boys tumbled off the bus, Narasimha, the camp in-charge called them all to assemble under a large mango tree outside a red-tiled house. He welcomed them and introduced himself and his three colleagues Ganesh, Vinod and John. He asked them to explore the place and return to the front veranda within 15 minutes.

Vinod then read out the room allotments and invited the boys to find a name for their group. The older boys Mahesh, Akram, Naresh, Arul and Feroz Shafique were in the bigger room. They called themselves the Tiger Group. Murugan, Chinna, Rajan, Dhanraj, Mahadev and Nanadalal were the 14-year-olds and they chose to call themselves Sachin Group (after the Indian cricketer). The younger ones were in two groups. Sultan, Amir, Vishnu, Bashan, Atul and Rashid Khan were the Rajdhani Group (a superfast train) and the youngest ones were the 11-year olds Sai Pradeep, Kushal, Shyam, Srinivas and Saleem. They chose to call themselves the Rajini Group after a famous film star. Each group was assigned one camp teacher. The teachers were to observe the boys in their groups closely to develop a deeper understanding of the child's need. The boys felt better that they had a group to call their own and an assigned 'Sir'. There was some quick banter about which name was better as they shifted into their rooms. There were camp cots and lockers in each room. It was quite luxurious compared to the Sathi shelter but somewhat like the government home. It was a traditional house with an open courtyard and rooms opening off verandas. The kitchen, baths and toilets were a separate block a bit away from the building. It had a garden and coconut trees all around and was set in the middle of a sugarcane farm.

The camp team had come a day earlier to organise the stores for the kitchen, other materials like clothes stationery and so on. They had seen and discussed the reports available about the children to identify the major problems in the group such as family, education, individual, addiction or social issues. In this group, they realised that substance use and stealing were the main issues.

They were wondering how they were going to address the stealing issue and made a note to talk to Father George Kollashany,
the resourceful guide for all camp facilitators in Sathi. Vinod had
a few ideas that he wanted to try. Narasimha briefed the local
cook about the routines she had to manage. Ganesh had checked
out the water supply position and then spoken to the watchman
about power cuts in the locality. John had visited the local police
station and informed them about the camp. The police station
was already aware of Sathi's work because they had used the
same place for camps earlier.

Soon the boys reassembled. Narasimha and Ganesh got them
to play some games and the boys got to know each other a little
better. One surprise was that some of the boys knew one other
well. It turned out that Rashid Khan and Mahesh had met each
other in a children's home in Chennai. Of course the whole group
from the local children's home knew each other well. There were
also friendships from the platform. Some boys stayed quiet while
others were all chatter and energy. Some of them were busy
getting to know their room mates. The staff had taken care to
distribute two or three boys from the government children's home
across the rooms. They had also taken care to keep the younger
ones in together.

The camp teachers got busy. Most of the boys could read and
write and the staff decided to introduce the work book method
where each child was given a scrap book to document their own
learning with pictures and collages. The child could take this
book back and it would serve as a reminder of his work in the
camp. Vinod was assigned the task of being with the boys and
continued with the games. He was keeping a sharp eye out for any
rough behaviour or attempts at sneaking out or running away.
This period of settling in is, perhaps, the toughest patch in running the camp. John had taken on the responsibility of checking
with the boys how they experienced each session or activity. The
staff team was all set by lunch time. After lunch the boys rested
for a little while.

Narasimha gathered the entire group in the courtyard and
spoke a bit about the purpose of the camp—the daily routine and
the general norms of behaviour. He expressed hope that they will

be good to each other without fighting. He concluded by saying he wanted them to enjoy themselves and get an opportunity to learn and improve themselves. He invited questions and some of the boys aired their doubts. Arul wanted to know if they had to study. He had left home long ago and forgotten his schooling- he was from Tamil Nadu and vaguely remembered the Tamil script. Vinod used this opportunity to form some learning groups. There were some boys who were quite at ease with reading and writing. They were formed into one group. There were others like Arul with some schooling though were hazy about their alphabet and numbers. There were a few boys who had never been to school. Vinod had soon organised them for their study time. There was some relief all round when they heard that their lessons would only last two hours every morning. They went out and played cricket and came back at dusk. They sat around in a large circle. The staff invited the boys to talk about anything they wanted and soon there was an animated discussion comparing the camp and the children's home.

Settling In

The children discovered their routine on the second day. Wake-up time was 6 am. Yoga and meditation followed. After a bath and breakfast they could relax. There were activities organised for them till lunch. After a brief nap post lunch, they went out to play games like cricket and *kabbadi*. In the evening, they gathered for a group meeting. When Narasimha called for a volunteer to lead the children's meeting there was some surprise. Soon a list emerged as to who would lead the meeting on which day. All of them would have to take turns. Similarly each group chose a leader. This leader was in charge of the other boys in his room. He also made sure that the room was kept in good order. The leader also looked for any problems that his members may have and reported them to the staff. The children also wanted leaders to take care of food and sports. Again it was agreed that these responsibilities will be rotated over the span of the camp.

Slowly the boys began to adapt to this routine. Vishnu did not mind the Yoga bit but felt tortured when asked to sit for meditation. He wondered how the other boys could sit with eyes shut. Many of them missed cigarettes, *ghutka* and solution and were irritable and ready to snap. During the games session on Wednesday one senior boy persuaded two others to run away and they disappeared into the sugarcane fields. A sudden barking of stray dogs alerted Vinod who was organising the boys into cricket teams. They were located and brought back. Narasimha spoke to them kindly for a long time. He offered to drop them back if they wanted to return to their old ways. He also explained why they should try to give up these substances and shared Sathi's experiences with other boys in earlier camps. Other boys were closely observing the whole situation. The big boys looked a bit shaken but were eventually ready to rejoin the group. Later that evening, the incident was discussed by all the boys in their meeting. They sat in smaller groups so that all could talk and review what happened that day.

There was some trouble the next day too. John found some boys smoking in the backyard. They were quite defiant and looked ready to fight. The staff team was calm but firm. Shyam, though very young, was one of those caught smoking. Vishnu went up to him later and tried to reason with him. Shyam just ignored him. In the group meeting that evening, many boys were angry. There were other boys who tried to calm them and finally Narasimha spoke for a while and explained the purpose and the pattern of the camp. The younger boys found it easier to go on with other activities. In the mornings, they could paint, read aloud, sing and act out small plays on various themes.

A counsellor began coming every day and talking to the boys who were willing to share information. Soon the routine was set and the boys were beginning to enjoy the yoga and meditation sessions and slowly forget their need for different stimulants. Two doctors arrived on the fifth day and completed a medical examination. The staff members were relieved when the visitors declared that all the boys were in good health.

When the camp staff Nagaraj, Vinod, Ganesh and John sat together to review the first week, it was clear that some boys were finding it very difficult to settle in.

Murugan (aged about 14) was not ready to settle in. He was brought from the Sathi shelter on the third day of the camp. He was found in the station and spoke only his mother tongue, Tamil. He said he had studied up to the ninth standard and that he had run away several times. Unlike the others he felt he was pushed into the camp by Sathi and claimed he wasn't properly informed about the camp. He felt alone and left out of conversations in Hindi or Kannada, the languages the others used. He had no desire to go home and wanted to earn his living and lead a free life on the platform. He fought with the other children and at the same time complained that they were not friendly with him. Shyam was one of the youngest and also difficult to handle. He continued to remain closed and resisted efforts of others to befriend him and was caught smoking beedis.

As they slipped into the second week, the routine seemed comfortable: Yoga, *dhyana*, breakfast, classes, lunch, nap, games, group discussion, dinner and bed. Sometimes, they worked in two or three small groups; the staff read to them from story books and asked them what they thought of an incident or a situation. Very often the children were able to link up these stories with their own lives. One evening the boys watched a video on the harmful effects of smoking and chewing tobacco. This was rather frightening for the children and many decided to give up these habits quite readily once they knew all this. They also recalled the words of the doctor about health and nutrition. Most of them had never thought about it earlier. The boys shared their views on what they heard during the group meetings. Often, the older ones were scornful of what was said and refused to take it all seriously. Some boys came out powerfully against such bad habits.

Arul, a 16-year-old had run away four times and now stayed in the government children's home and did not like his own family home. At the same time he was careful to stay away from harmful habits like substance abuse on the railway stations. He spoke up in group sessions about the need to break out of such habits and supported the staff on this aspect.

Similarly, Vishnu too voiced his fears about the use of such harmful substances. Some science experiments were conducted by a visitor to the camp. The children found it exciting and even the scornful ones were gripped. Even within the first 10 days they were able to notice the improvement in their own health and stamina.

Family and Home

Slowly the topic of home crept into the group discussions. Children who had been very proud of their platform deeds, often imagined, now began to speak of their homes—some boastfully, others rather hesitantly.

Dhanraj, a fourteen-year-old, from Chikmagalur spoke about his family—he is dark-skinned and his family likes his fairer brother better. His parents stole and threw blame on the boy and Dhanraj had thought of ending his own life several times.

There were some boys who were eager to explore the world and have fun. They did not spare much thought for their parents and other loved ones at home.

Rashid Khan, a twelve-year-old living in Tumkur, left home with a few friends to see the sea at a Cochin. He got detached from his group of friends somewhere along the way and was sent to the government home in Chennai. He escaped from there and managed to reach Bangalore station. He was rescued by BOSCO, presented to the CWC and admitted into the government home in Bangalore. He seemed unmoved when some boys admitted to missing their homes.

Basha wept bitterly about how he missed his mother who was no longer alive. The camp teachers and others tried to comfort him. Mallesh was one of the boys deeply affected by Basha's story. He too had lost his mother and had left home because his step-mother had blamed him for stealing and his father had not supported him. Vishnu came down to earth and changed his earlier stories—the first one about a powerful political family and the second one about an orphan left with an uncaring brother. He admitted that he had come away just for fun and had done this several times earlier. He was also touched and moved by Basha's tears.

Feroze Shafique, a fifteen-year-old from Chitradurga, was quite clear he wanted to be back home and fit in there. He had, in fact, been reunited with his family by Sathi and his parents sent him to the camp so that he could overcome his many bad habits like stealing mobile phones. He had earlier run away with an older cousin, got caught in the Chennai railway station and had been repatriated through the Chennai and Bangalore children's homes. He shared his whole story and declared that he had come to the camp only to go past this unfortunate phase in his life.

Many shared stories of their problems on the platform—abuse, police harassment, teasing, stealing, sheer hard work and the dangers and suffering. One boy talked about losing his friend—he had fallen off a train. Others showed scars of their own wounds and described the injuries some friends had suffered. As the second week ended, at least half the boys were beginning to speak about their deeper feelings and share their insecurities. Vinod introduced the concept of '*deepa*' or a flame spreading light and driving away darkness. He also spoke about knowledge as against ignorance and courage as against fear, during the meditation classes. Many of them found it very soothing to sit quietly together watching the gentle flame of the oil lamp that evening. Sai Pradeep sang a *bhajan* (devotional song) softly and the others joined in. This gradually became a part of their evening group session with the Muslim boys bringing in Urdu songs. Topics introduced for group discussion were somewhat uncomfortable at times. Stealing, fighting, solution use, sexuality, love and intimacy were all discussed. For the boys who were struggling with such issues, they heard a variety of perspectives from their peers as well as the camp teachers. As they were beginning to speak the truth, many boys had to acknowledge some of their own mistakes which triggered their exit from home. Some were remorseful and others defiant. However, they were all fearful that their families would not accept them readily even if they were contacted by Sathi. This fear of rejection was very big, especially with those who had runaway many times. Some of them felt guilty that they were now habituated to many bad habits which they would like to keep hidden from their families, especially their mothers and sisters.

Salman, for example, was now regretful about his misbehaviour. He was merely 13 when he had got involved with a girl in the neighbourhood. His parents were shocked and the first reaction was a severe beating. Community elders advised the parents to send him to a Madrassa for a religious education with suitable discipline. He was already defiant when he went there and he escaped from there at first opportunity. He was reluctant to check if his family would have him back and did not really want to go back to the government children's home which had sent him to the Sathi camp.

In the meanwhile, Dhanraj changed his story when he realised that his parents were actually on their way to meet him. His family was poor and they did love him very much. He had run away because they wanted him to focus on his school.

Other boys were ready to talk about their broken families or uneasy relationships with step-parents. One boy did not approve of his mother's second marriage after his father's death, though she cared for him. Some had lost their parents and had runaway from relatives who were their guardians.

Preparing For the Return

A psychiatrist came for three days in the morning to take the boys through sessions on life skills like self confidence, communication, empathy, critical thinking, creativity, problem-solving and decision-making. Both staff and children found the sessions very useful and they could think of how to apply these ideas to choose their path ahead.

Some of the children began to share details of their home; the staff were finding enough data to establish contact. Other boys seemed happier but not ready to talk about home. As they progressed into the third week the messages to the children about the importance of home and family were not so subtle anymore. The children were now mostly free from dependence on stimulants. The regular routine brought in a sense of physical well-being. They became more alive to the natural beauty and the greenery around them. They remembered to sing softer gentler songs. They could play without fighting. They took turns to handle responsibilities and the staff breathed a little easier. By the end of the third week, 11 addresses had been traced and the parents invited to meet their children at the close of the camp. Four boys had been sent by their families any way. The road ahead was still clouded for the remaining six.

Most of the stories in the classes were about the relationships within the family and with teachers and other role models, the children reflected on how the different characters in the stories showed their devotion for their God, their country, their teachers and their parents. This gradually took them in to their own memories of how their own parents have shown affection and taken care of them. Discussions were around the roles parents play and the benefits of having a family. They also discussed how they could cope with problems, handle anger and aggression and adopt problem-solving techniques. They discussed coping with hardships, setting examples for others and becoming recognized in society by their achievements with the help of stories and songs. A lady who was a volunteer for Sathi came for three days and they created role plays and enacted them together. The boys were fantastic mimics and they could bring alive the different characters they had met in their adventures and their emotional turmoil too.

As the fourth week began, most of the boys were ready to go home. They found that the themes for the stories during the last week were slightly different. They were mostly real life stories of individuals who had overcome hardships and adverse conditions to become renowned people. Children also shared personal experiences, giving examples of successful people whom they knew. They began to recognise and discuss their own personal ambitions, problems they had faced and the ways in which they could handle and overcome these problems to achieve their goals. The metaphor of the child as a flower, liked by all, cared for by God, spreading happiness and joy like the flower spreads its scent, was introduced for meditation.

Children realised that the camp would end soon. Some of them were suddenly anxious. They really had no home they wished to go back to. The platform or the government homes were not options anymore. The camp staff members were able to identify the further course of action for most of the boys. There were four boys sent to the camp by parents. Fortunately, all the four boys had indeed changed their attitudes and habits and were ready to rejoin the family. For example, Mahadev had hated his family and even changed his name to give up his older identity. He was given to stealing and used tobacco. He left home when his neighbour falsely accused him of stealing money and his father did not defend him. He had been reunited with his family by Sathi earlier, but continued to behave badly. In the course of a follow-up phone call, Sathi suggested that he may benefit from the camp and the family then enrolled him. He had undergone a change of heart in the camp and was eager now to return.

Fifteen other boys had shared their addresses and the family members had been contacted.

In Sathi's assessment, ten families were fit to offer a good home for their boys. The situation was a bit complex in the other five cases even though the parents were eager to have the child back.

Murugan, who had begun as a trouble-maker, settled down and gave complete details of his family to the counsellor. It was clear that the family was repeatedly sending him to distant places for work. Murugan wishes to study and improve his prospects and had good academic skills. The camp staff felt that he could return to regular school after a bridge course to cover the gap in schooling. The family sounded happy that he was found, but claimed they were too poor to travel all the way from their village in interior Tamil Nadu. It was decided that a staff member would travel with him and personally verify the situation. If the home could support schooling, Sathi could supplement their resources with a scholarship. If this seemed unlikely, Murugan could go to the government home through the CWC.

Arul's story was a little different. His biological father had deserted his mother. She then developed a relationship with another partner and Arul did not like that. The mother was very eager to take him back and after much discussion it was decided that Arul would go to a hostel for vocational training and visit his mother for vacations.

Basha's story was also very complex. His aunt and uncle arrived and they were full of concern. They disclosed that the mother was murdered by the father who was then sent to jail. The boy had suffered deep trauma. They wanted him back and Sathi agreed and offered to find counselling support for the child.

Some boys like Shyam were silent and would not share anything about their family. Shyam was willing to go to the government home and enrol in the local school there. Sathi would continue to be his friend in need because they were working within the children's home. The camp team was happy that a suitable way was found for all the children in the camp.

Three boys were going to join the Don Bosco vocational training institution and stay in contact with their families. In two of these cases, the families were engaged in begging and it was therefore considered unsuitable that the boys be sent home. Two were going to the government children's home. In one case, the nearest relatives located were the grandparents, who were themselves in need of care and support.

Clues For Better Parenting

Parents began to arrive even two days before camp closure. Those who had sent their boys were eager to see what impact the camp had made. Their boys were eager to tell them that they would refrain from stealing and unruly behaviour. For some others, it was a deeply emotional reconnecting after years of separation. As parents came to the camp they met most of the boys; they met other parents too. They observed the children at their games, work, play and interaction. They shared their feelings among themselves.

The camp staff and a counsellor spent a good bit of time talking to them about how they should help the child stabilise at home. Very often, there was wide variance between the versions of the parents and the versions of the children about the causes for the child leaving home. A dialogue on this was the most important starting point. They also briefed each family about how their child had lived on the platform and the changes seen in the camp. A plan for the child's future was drawn up. In a few cases, the family needed financial support to send the child to school. This too was noted.

In the course of meetings, parents were provided some guidelines to stabilise their children. They were advised first to spend time with the child and demonstrate their love for the child. Listening to the child carefully and answering questions patiently and acknowledging his positive qualities were important. Parents were also advised to accept their son as he is, refrain from comparisons and have realistic expectations. Most importantly, they were advised to trust the child, convey love through touch and avoid embarrassing him before others. The parents in the group were already well aware that corporal punishments, anger and scolding were counter-productive with these children.

The camp closing ceremony was very moving. Most of the boys were happy. The parents were uniformly happy. The chief guests were the superintendent of the government home and the police chief from the railway station. Each child was formally entrusted to the family and the boys put up a brief cultural programme where the highlight was a play scripted by them on the theme of the lost child retuning home. For the camp staff it was a fulfilling moment. The boys took fond leave of them—some were in tears. Some of the boys volunteered to help the staff pack and organise the return journey. Before leaving the camp location the staff completed their own reflection on what went well and what did not. Using their weekly observation record, they completed the 'before and after' report on the children and recorded the care plan finalised for each of them.

Views About the Camps

Basavaraj Shali of Sathi recalls the origin of the camps. It began as a day picnic and soon became a week-long training conducted at MAYA, an NGO in Bangalore. The camps brought lot of change in the children's behaviour in weaning them away from the bad habits of platform life. Topics and themes got added and the period was extended to a month. Father George Kollashany helped to develop the activities and trained the staff. BOSCO, APSA, Saathi Mumbai, Balaprafulta and Baltejasu were early partners who extended these camps to many places. Over time, the structure has stabilised and new techniques and methods have been added. The staff members of Sathi are now well prepared to take the lead to innovate. It is difficult to find a name for these camps. They were referred to initially as de-addiction and home placement camps. Slowly this has now changed to reduction of substance abuse and home orientation camps. The camps are so uniquely tailored to the requirements that it is, in our view, best to call them Sathi Camps.

The basic design of the camp was created by Dr Shekhar Sheshadri (NIMHANS) in 2003–04, based on his interactions with the children before going to the camps and also after the camps. The camps themselves were organised on the conceptual principle of a transit experience that bridges the gap between platform life and a positive home experience. The camp offers a specific routine, structured to suit the child's physical and emotional well being instead of the railway time-table and station cleaning routines. The child is supervised kindly but firmly and there are many opportunities created for reflection and sharing. The child jumps from one challenge to another on the platform constantly facing fear, hunger and danger. In the camp, there is safety and the child is not exploited or abused in any manner. Harmful substances are not available and the child is again free to discover simple pleasures through games, music drama and creative self expression. Very importantly, the child is expected to take responsibility for the management of the camp and collaborate with other children as well as adults. This design addresses the chaos of platform life and brings in some regularity and stability gradually. The regime is clearly there but gently held in place and prepares the child to fit into a disciplined routine back home or in other institutions.

The camp has continued to be the most challenging and satisfying service that Sathi provides for the children over the years. It is highly specialised, and not easily replicated by other NGOs. The impact is clearly established. The basic indicator of Sathi's success is that the most children remain with the family after the reunion (see Table 1.2).

Given the fact that the children at camps are usually habituated to their free roaming life, holding them back home is a challenge. Therefore the retention rate of 90 per cent achieved through camps is indeed remarkable compared to the 95 per cent achieved in the easier cases directly reunited from shelters. This provides the empirical evidence to establish the efficacy of the camps. Sathi continues to improve the methodology with guidance from experts like Dr Shekhar Seshadri, Dr Sanjeev, Dr Ramachandran and Father George Kollashany. Father George is now heading an action research project to integrate counselling methods in the camp design and adapted it to children from Government homes. It is a continuing challenge to find and train the staff to run the camps.

It is sometimes said that the design has not been revisited or critically evaluated since it was formalised in 2003. Sathi is proud of the camp methodology but is yet to develop in-house expertise to design related and new services of similar impact and intensity. Critics feel that it should go beyond such dependence on external expertise. It has also been pointed out that Sathi is not adequately prepared for emergencies and there are huge risks involved in running these camps.

The other issue raised is about the pressure put on a child who is emotionally vulnerable to somehow fit back into the family. Though Sathi makes efforts to assess the family and maintain contact with the child it has no programme to offer to those children who cannot readjust. It also has no programme to counsel or work with the parents and elders to support the child better.

Sathi camps have been highly effective in getting children out of bad habits like tobacco and solution. Unlike adults, children seem to shake off these habits far more easily. Sathi's courage in taking the risk of organising these camps without any medication for the children has paid off. At the same time this has raised many doubts, especially in the minds of funding agencies, and this aspect too needs highlighting. Sathi has experimented with offering camps for children from urban slums because of the rampant substance abuse among them. While the camps themselves have worked well, the assumption that the family is caring and will take good care of their children does not hold true in urban slums. Sathi has preferred to keep its focus on runaway children on railway platforms and their reunification with families. It hopes that such work can spread in urban slums through partner support.

The government homes are another important niche for offering the camps. Sathi is set to explore this much further in the coming years.

Chapter Seven

Homecoming*

Vishnu's Return

Vishnu's return was 'breaking news' and all aspects were discussed in many corners of the village through the day. Vishnu was certainly happy to return home. Suddenly, he began to feel anxious. He felt many eyes on him as he walked down the street with his parents. He was beginning to wonder what they thought of him—and wishing he had been better behaved. A cheerful young voice rang out greeting him and he was soon he was surrounded by a group of friends. His mother, noticing the throng, nodded and he hung back to chat though his parents moved ahead. They had many questions and he was eager to tell his story. They agreed to meet in the evening after school.

His grandmother and little sister had been waiting eagerly for him and they hugged him warmly as he entered. A little dog ran around him excitedly and he realised it was the pup he had found starving in a ditch and brought home. He ran to the backyard and the cows were still in their stall. Suddenly, he felt completely free of all tension. He could smell the hot *dosas* his grandmother was making and went in quickly for breakfast.

The old ladies of the village who walked to the little Ganesh temple at 10 am, talked about similar events in the village over the last few decades. They were all happy that the tracing of the children is easier today. There were tales told of black magic, kidnapping and rackets which harmed these children and made them to work in stone quarries or as beggars.

---

*Details provided in italics are based on field work and interviews by the authors. Names have been changed to provide confidentiality.

It was the topic of the day in the teachers' common room at lunch time. Opinion was divided. A child like Vishnu needed a firm hand and a thrashing. Look at all the trouble for the parents. There were some murmurs that disagreed. Vishnu's father was in fact too strict. Anyway some of them decided to talk to their students and advice them. Vishnu's class teacher, a kind-hearted woman, decided to keep a close watch on the boy and help him catch up with the lessons he had missed.

The mothers' group discussed the story and issues animatedly during the self-help group meeting at 2 pm. The costs incurred in tracing the child, the other parents they met at Sathi, how boys are so difficult to handle besides Vishnu's mother saw and heard in the whole trip. In the evening Vishnu's father met his friends at the tea shop in the village square. His friends were happy for him. Many remembered that they had young boys wanting to run away too. Some shared details of similar incidents that they had heard of. Vishnu's father told them about his own realisation—he had been too strict with his son. Today's children are different and expect more from parents.

The children who met Vishnu to play with him had many other questions. Nobody asked, 'Why did you come back?' but clearly he was given a hero's welcome. And Vishnu really enjoyed describing cities, trains, friends, enemies, policemen, fights, girls, crime, movies and cigarettes. But soon he stopped this line of bragging and very soberly described the dangers of the platform and strongly advised his friends not to leave the safety of the home and the village. Certainty the benefit of wisdom he gained at the camp!

The family settled for the night, though Vishnu was still too excited to sleep. The many images and impressions of the last few months swirled around in his head. He decided to call some of his camp buddies the next day—he wondered what happened to the three or four boys who had no home to go to. He decided to call them the next day just as he was nodding off.

Vishnu's escapades ended happily for him. His village came together to keep a gentle watch on him and very soon he was set on his school work and took an active interest in social studies.

Sathi's Choices

Vishnu's story is perhaps the 'typical' Sathi story. The child has strayed but can be guided back fairly easily. There were others who were less fortunate. They found it hard to accept their situation and there were a few who did run away again. But the majority of them have managed to stay on and rebuild their lives. There are also a few children with no homes they can be sent back to. Sathi then becomes the agent to find the right place for them which will offer the safety and access to education or vocational training suited for them.

Vishnu's friend Shyam continued to remain closed and aloof for the first two weeks in the camp. He was clear that he had no home he could go back to. His story was that his parents died when he was young and his elder brother had driven him out of the house listening to the tales his wife carried to him.

With guidance and counselling in the camp, he expressed a desire to go to a vocational training school. Sathi was happy to arrange for his admission into a BOSCO facility nearby. In the camp he gradually opened out to others, especially when he discovered that others too had similar or worse situations in their homes. He was not using tobacco or solution and was orderly and well behaved through the camp. The staff was sure that he could adapt to the vocational training school.

Akram, another 15-year-old in the camp, had left home after stealing Rs 22,000 (US$ 440) which he managed to fritter away when he reached the city. He was afraid to face his mother and elder brother. He had lost his father when young and his elder brother beat him up mercilessly when he found that he was into bad habits and stealing. His mother was old and frail and depended on her elder son.

Akram was moved by the stories and discussions about the child's responsibility to the mother. When the family was contacted the elder brother was very angry and did not want to take back the boy into his care. Akram had missed out several years of schooling and Sathi has found a vocational training course for him, which specially deals with children who are mildly delinquent or prone to conflict with the law.

The story of Mallesh a 17-year old was a situation where the family is ready to take back the child but the child is adamant.

Mallesh felt very angry with his father who had taken a second wife. They all lived together under one roof. He had stolen some money and his father had scolded him and reported this to the school.

He continued to be very angry with his father and refused to go home. Clearly, the child had not worked through his emotions and taken ownership for his part in the whole issue, namely stealing. The major change the camp brought about was in his attitude towards his studies. He wished to go to school and continue his education. He was referred to another NGO, APSA which offers bridge schooling. The child's behaviour is problematic even though the family is supportive. This happens in six per cent of the cases according to the analysis.

There are other cases like Murugan. The child had very clearly been sent into bonded labour repeatedly. Initially the child was reluctant to return and even resented the fact that he had been brought to remote camp. Gradually he changed his mind and the family was located.

Sathi visited his family and assessed the situation. They assured Sathi that they would not force him into work. Since he had studied so far in Tamil medium it was not feasible for Sathi to find a suitable hostel with all the facilities in Bangalore or Raichur. Sathi has offered the family financial support to enable Murugan to continue his education. The plan is to follow up every month for six months.

Reunions through Shelters

Similar complexity does arise when considering what to do with some of the children who are brought to the shelters. There are a few children who appear to emerge unscathed from a spell of platform life.

Vasudev comes from a middle-class home where he is well cared for and the emphasis is on education. He left home one day because he felt like it and wandered across several railway stations such as Mumbai, Chennai, Hyderabad, Raichur, Dharwad and Goa. He finally came to Bangalore and was working as a luggage porter to earn for his needs.

Sathi located him as 'new on the platform'. When he was brought to the shelter, he shared details of his platform spell and was reunited with his family. He keeps in touch with Sathi. He was safe throughout this span of nine months and learnt many things by observing life on the platform. He had missed a good part of his tenth class teaching and yet managed to clear the Secondary School Certificate examination. He has gone on to qualify himself in computers and found a job and lives happily with his parents and elder brother. In retrospect, his platform stay seems like a backpacking holiday that any adolescent might embark on. He has developed confidence and can manage his own needs anywhere at any time.

Prakash lived in a village in Karnataka and his parents were daily wage earners. He was keen on his schooling and asked for money to buy a notebook one evening. It was vacation time and Prakash wanted to prepare ahead for the next term. His parents had no money that evening and his father's comment, 'Go and earn it yourself!' bothered him so much that he walked off in a huff. Reaching the station, he hesitated, got on to a train and got off at Bangalore. He managed to earn Rs 150 as a porter. Not knowing what to do next, he sat and cried.

A Sathi person approached him and he cried even more saying that he had 'lost his mother and missed the train'. He was scared of the stranger and was finally convinced by the Sathi identity card. He stayed two days in shelter and finally gave the phone number of an affluent neighbour in his village and the family was contacted. Recognising this as a simple case, Sathi escorted him home and gave him ₹1,000 for books (in kind). Having recovered from this experience, he finished school and went on to work in a cooperative bank in Bangalore, sharing room with four others. He is also at peace with his family and peers.

Peter is now 20 years old. When he was 16, he wanted to be a driver but his dad, a coconut dealer, wanted him to study. He stole Rs 1,000 from his dad and walked to the station. Though initially hesitant, he boarded the train to Bangalore.

He was found on the platform by Sathi who brought him to the shelter. He lied initially that he was from Tirupati. A week later, he realised he was better off at home, and gave his telephone number. Sathi counselled him and requested the father not to press too hard. He is now a qualified driver, earning ₹5,000 (US$ 100) a month.

Sometimes Sathi comes across special or differently-abled children who are in no position to divulge their personal details. The staff are on the lookout for clues all the time which may lead them to what they ultimately believe in—getting the child back home.

Rahim (12) looked very healthy physically but seemed a bit mentally unstable. He would just answer in gestures. All he would do was to imitate bus conductors who call out names of places. Sathi suspected he worked in a bus. He was sent with one of the staff to a bus stand. On seeing him, many bus drivers gathered and began asking where he had gone. Sathi learnt from them that he had worked in the bus station for two years. He was an errand boy for all the drivers. They would give him food to eat. They also told the staff that the boy's father was serving a murder sentence and mother was mentally unsound. The boy worked and slept in the bus stand.

The drivers would also make the boy drink while they drank alcohol so that he would not trouble them. This constant drinking at a very early age has hindered his mental growth and resulted in blurred speech.

When Sathi suggested they would rescue the boy and put him at the shelter or get him home, the bus drivers and conductors refused to let him go. Finally, when Sathi staff asked them to give it in writing that they are responsible for the boy, they agreed to let him go. The boy was later taken to the shelter. He began talking slowly. He was put in the Sathi camp. He suffered an epileptic attack due to withdrawal symptoms. At the end of the fourth week he was willing to go to school or back home. He has a grandma who wants him to be with her and help her in her farm. Sathi took the case to the CWC and they arranged that the child was sent to a special home run by an NGO.

Sometimes sending the child back home is no option for Sathi. When Sathi came across an eleven-year-old repeated runaway from his home and the shelter, they were in a fix. While talking to him one of the staff, a Muslim, suggested if he would like to go to a Madrassa and the boy was willing to go. He liked being with his community, speaking the same language. So Sathi agreed to send him there and continues to be in contact with him.

In some cases, the child's parent admits him/her to the government home voluntarily.

In one such case, the child's father was no more and mother remarried. She had three more children through her second marriage. The step-father did not want to keep the boy. He ran away repeatedly. They accused him of spoiling the family's name and he ran away because he was taunted and did not feel loved. He was admitted into the government home by the family.

The boy was admitted to one of the Sathi camps at the Government Home. After the camp, the mother and the step-father were invited to meet the child and Sathi staff made them understand how important it is for the child to be in contact with the family.

The mother agreed and now they are trying to leave the child with his maternal grandmother, while the step-father has agreed to pay his school fee if he is willing to go to school.

Sathi has also experienced that runaways need not necessarily be from the poorer sections of the society.

Nilesh, an 11-year-old, had run away because he had cut his own hair to imitate a film star. His mother had disapproved of his act, slapped him and yelled, 'Get out of here'. He had done so. He had run to the station, aiming to go to the family native place, Chitoor, in Andhra Pradesh.

Something went amiss and he was found at Bangalore by Sathi. He was taken to the shelter for three days. Initially, he concocted stories about where his family home was. Slowly, he began playing with other children. Over time, he realised it was better to go home and gave the right contact number and went home. Nilesh's father works in the accounts department in a public sector undertaking. His mother is a housewife and they live in a pleasant flat. They speak good English and he was studying in a private English medium school where his parents paid an annual fee of ₹50,000 (US$ 1,000). Nilesh has promised never to run away from home and he is willing to talk to other children in shelters and homes and tell them it's better to go home.

Sathi's Model on Runaway Children

Sathi has found it useful to take a stance that running away is a stage in an adolescent's life. This has enabled them to build a programme to directly address the emotional state of the children they meet. Very often the adolescent boy or girl experiences anger and frustration in their families. They struggle to find their own identity and it is irksome to be checked by well meaning adults at every turn. It is even worse when the adults are not so well meaning or trustworthy. The world outside seems alluring and a hasty decision to leave the home can be triggered by a small incident.

Sathi avoids any judgement on the family and takes stand that in most cases the family does love the child and the problems arise from the lack of communication or expression of this love and care. Sathi also recognises the rapid changes in the emotional state of a child leaving home. The anger, frustration, pain or just curiosity that triggers the act of running away soon vanishes, to be replaced by fear and anxiety. A few days on the platform and a few friendly invitations from the boys already there are enough to build the confidence of the child that he can survive. The fear and anxiety gives place to a sense of confidence and excitement over the new context. Depending on the friendships and associations formed in this stage, the child can get into a state of complete rebellion and experiment with the many attractions and temptations. The transition to maturity and adulthood is a move beyond this rather dysfunctional state of absolute freedom. The value of relationships and family becomes important again as the child tires of this false freedom and recognises the inherent dangers. This cycle is observed everywhere and poverty and unfavourable circumstances aggravate these growth pangs.

Figure 7.1:
Teen Tantrums

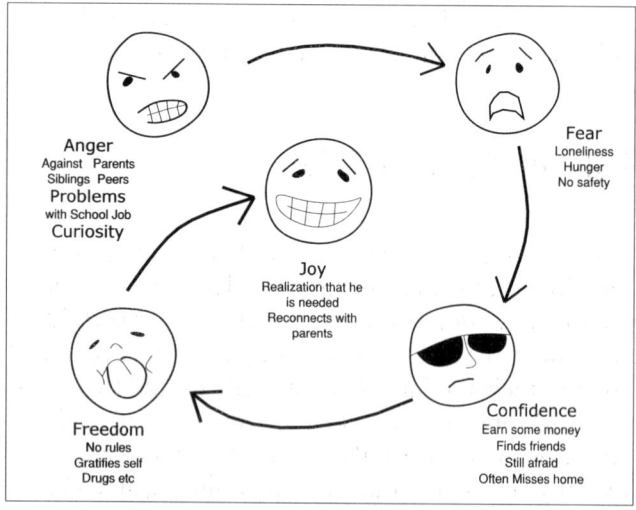

Source: Developed by author for Sathi in 2003.

Sathi's response matches the child's emotions and helps the child to reflect and go beyond the trap he is in. Most children arriving on the platform carry anger and fear from home and are in a state of shock when they see the conditions on the platform. The platform educators in Sathi are well aware of this and see it as their first task to calm these children. The outreach work reaches out to these lonely frightened boys and the shelter offers them a sense of physical safety and re-assurance about basic needs. The guidance available and the practical support to return home is adequate to meet the requirements of most of the children.

If the problems are deeper the Sathi camp helps the child re-examine how this freedom spoils their future. It leads to a family reunification or a longer term institutional arrangement.

Sathi find that the emotional journey is the same for children in government homes also. Therefore it has been able to adapt its methods quite effectively to that system also. In many ways this working model is quite different from the beliefs held by others.

Figure 7.2:
Sathi's Support

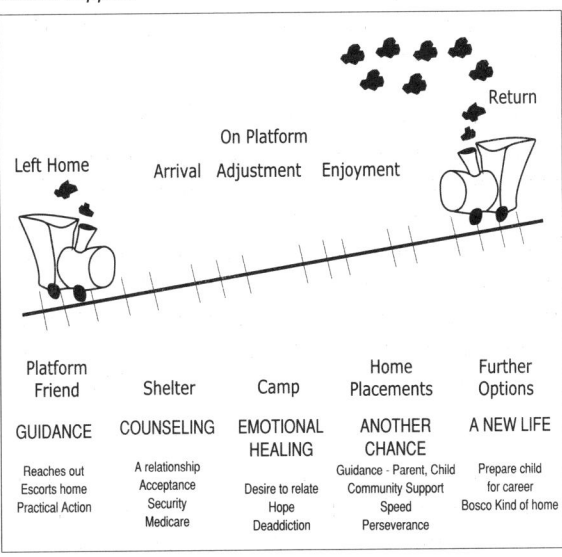

Follow-Up Measures

Sathi has continued to monitor how the children fare on their return home. Initially this was prompted by the criticism that Sathi merely puts pressure on the children to go back to an impossible situation. As it finds that most children indeed do stay back at home and seem happy, it has continued to research the question of why it works.

Sathi has tried to understand what children seek when they long for home. Interviews with children and young adults who are in institutions and group homes point to the emotional as well as physical aspects children expect. One major phrase which recurs is the feeling of freedom. Another is the feeling of being accepted for what one is. Children expect basic facilities, family members, safety to keep one's own things and a sense of routine. Understanding this first intuitively and then empirically, Sathi has designed the processes in shelters and camps. There is an emphasis on daily routine, gentle relationships with adults who accept children as they are, wholesome food and enough rest. All these are things missing on the platform.

Sathi continues to follow up with children who were reunited with their families on a regular basis. From time to time, Sathi staff actually visit the children and it is heartening to find that many indeed do stay at home.

Sathi met Santrupt (16) at the Bangalore railway station in November 2010. He had left home because his mother had scolded him and beaten him for being irregular at school. This was the seventh time he had run away. With counselling and guidance at the shelter, he recognised his mistakes and decided to make a change for the better. Sathi found that the family was financially stable and the parents were very keen that he should study. They were advised about the boy's change of heart and they agreed not to scold and beat him. (Field research by authors)

Sathi staff visited the home in February 2012, nearly a year and a half later. They met Santrupt and spoke with the family. The boy was about to complete his higher secondary school and he was looking forward to join his father's professional line. The mother was happy about her son's transformation. The boy still felt a little scared of his father, though he acknowledged that his parents had stopped scolding and beating him.

In this case the success can be attributed to the favourable family circumstances as well as the boy's change of heart. Not all families are so readily accepting of their own shortcomings and ready to change them. Financial security is another major issue.

Chandra (11) was found on the Bangalore platform in January 2006. He stayed at the shelter for nearly 10 days and was initially very troublesome. He responded to the counselling and shared details about his family. He said that he was afraid to return because he had been tending sheep and some other boys had thrown stones and injured the animals. The family was relieved to have received news about their son and his uncle reached the Sathi office immediately. His parents were wage labourers and had sold their cattle to search for their lost son.

Sathi staff visited the home in February 2012 and were happy to find Chandra at home, six years after the reunification. He was nearly 18 and well adjusted in the family. He did not resume his education since he was not interested and began working to help his family. The family acknowledged his changed behaviour and were hoping that he would one day buy land and become a farmer. One area of concern was his continued dependence on alcohol and drugs. The staff felt that they could have sent him to a camp before home placement to avoid this situation.

There are many such stories about the children and their families and these are shared here to just give a glimpse of how children go back and build their lives. The level of follow-up required is planned for each child and family based on the situation. A follow-up is usually a phone call. Sometimes if the phone does not work, a physical visit is undertaken. The frequency is usually a quarterly phone call. If the situation requires it, the calls are made every month. The child too has Sathi contact details and addressed post cards to use in case of need. Sathi has found that the reunification process works because of the strength of the emotional bonds which hold the child and its family together, particularly in rural and traditional communities. Sathi's research findings on why their approach works can be summarised in the following terms:

When the boy returns home, the emotional equations between the boy and the family have changed substantially. The family has become acutely aware that the boy is important for them. The boy has suffered the rough life outside and has begun to appreciate the emotional and other support that his family offers. Especially after the camp, the boy recognises that he has a duty and responsibility towards his family. Sathi ensures that parents spend at least a day to understand the camp and the specific issues which drove their child out of the house and kept him there for many months. When the child returns to the streets after these efforts it is usually because he does not see any change or improvement in the way the family deals with him. There are families which are not ready to make any extra effort to reach out to the child.

Another issue arises when the child continues to behave aggressively or steal, specially because of the continued need to use substances like tobacco or solution. The efforts of the camp are very relevant for these children because they control their aggression, reduce substance use and stop stealing or lying. When parents report such problems during the follow-up of children home-placed through the shelter, Sathi offers to include such children in a camp so that the problem is addressed at a deeper level.

There are also instances where the child has been through a very traumatic experience, either at home or on the platform. In such situations, Sathi takes care to inform the family or the institution and sets up some arrangement for continued counselling for the child after the camp. If the family has problems in supporting the education of the child, Sathi offers financial support.

Most importantly, Sathi decides on the frequency of follow-ups needed and calls the more complex cases every month and other once in three months. This provides an opportunity to know how the child is and offer any tangible support that the parent or child might require.

Despite all these efforts, there are children who return to the streets. Sathi has learnt to accept that this will happen, and works hard to reduce that number as far as possible.

Chapter Eight

Spreading the Lessons of Experience

Sathi as a Social Enterprise

Sathi, like any organisation, believes in its 'product', that is, the process of getting runaway children home, and wants more 'clients' to receive and benefit from it. This is true for any type of organisation, be it a car manufacturer, a hotel or a theatre, or, for that matter, a religion, or a political party. But, and critically, Sathi is a 'social enterprise'. This term is over-used and misused. If it means anything, it should surely only be used to describe an institution which not only believes in what it does, but also believes that its own growth and success is much less important than the degree to which its objectives are achieved, irrespective of which institution achieves them. Ford wants more cars to be sold, but it wants them to be Ford cars. Coca-Cola wants more people to drink cola drinks, but it wants them to drink Coca-Cola, not Pepsi. Sathi wants more runaway railway children to go home, but it does not mind which institution gets them there, so long as it is done sensitively and humanely. This focus on the overall objective is surely a critical hallmark of a genuine social enterprise.

Sathi uses a number of different approaches in its efforts to broaden its impact, to reach more of the thousands of children on railway station platforms and to get as many of them back to their families as possible. It has to work with other institutions, beyond its own staff and offices, in three fundamentally different ways.

First, and most obviously, Sathi collaborates with institutions which play some part in Sathi's own direct function of getting railway platform children home, such as the police and railway staff and children's institutions.

Secondly, Sathi tries to spread the word and thus attempts to influence others to adopt its own policy of putting family reunion at the top of the agenda. This is done through the media, through Sathi's own annual reports and other publications and research studies, and we hope through this book too.

Thirdly, which is often the most difficult, Sathi attempts to extend its methods to more places, and thus to help more children, by forming partnerships with local NGOs which are familiar with local languages and systems. Sathi works with them to extend their activities into reuniting children with their families along with their other programmes, such as platform or street schools, or children's residential homes. This is analogous to franchising in a commercial context.

A private for-profit company will try to capture a larger market share to consolidate its position. Similarly, large and aggressive NGOs which want to grow might choose to scale up either 'horizontally', by starting operations in more cities, perhaps even internationally, or 'vertically', by itself carrying out more of the total operation. Sathi restricts itself to the specific parts of the process which are critical to its vision of getting as many children as possible to go home, as soon as possible. Hence, Sathi has its own staff on railway platforms, and its own short-term shelters near stations where it operates. This is sufficient for the majority of the children whom Sathi contacts, as we have seen; they can either be sent home or in rare cases enrolled in government children's homes or similar institutions.

Collaborating with Platform Stakeholders

Sathi's work requires substantial collaboration and co-operation with the two different systems of railway police, the railway staff themselves and with other NGOs on the same station and who may be 'competing' for the same runaway children. This is not easy.

Sathi works closely with the railway authorities. Runaway children are a distraction and an irritant to managers and lower level staff whose task is to run what is perhaps the world's largest and most complex railway system. At the most basic level, Sathi staff needs permission to work on platforms and identity cards to prove their *bona fides*, not only to the police and others, but to the children whom they contact, and to other travellers. In all the stations, the police have set up special systems to maintain a daily register of all the children with whom NGO staff or the police themselves come into contact. Some station managements have also allocated small rooms or other spaces to Sathi, on or adjacent to the platforms. Sathi staff can bring children to these places as soon as they have contacted them for a decent conversation uninterrupted by the noise and bustle of the platform. The local railway authorities, acting within their discretion, help in organising travel for children and for Sathi staff escorting them home or for parents or other family members who come to collect them. This support is offered because of the goodwill built up and nurtured by the Sathi teams in each location. Sathi also receives and takes help from the travelling ticket examiners (TTEs), who are perhaps best positioned to spot and report runaway children because they are on trains and can notice children who board long distance trains without adult escort or support. Sathi has, therefore, been making attempts to include modules on child protection and awareness in the training programmes that the railways organise for them.

In addition to the railway's own management and staff, two different police forces operate in all major railway stations in India .The GRP (Government Railway Police) and RPF (Railway Protection Force) patrols are present on the platform and on the trains. There are a few significant differences between the GRP and RPF. The RPF comes under the control of the Central Government and is committed to the safety of railway property. The GRP, controlled by the state government, is responsible for the prevention and detection of crime and ensuring law and order. They supplement each other for professional, efficient, transparent and passenger-friendly policing. Most children who run away and reach these stations have already learned to be inconspicuous.

The only children whom the police are likely to watch are those who live on the platforms, by begging, stealing or working outside the law as porters, vendors or in other forms of employment or self-employment. To the police, these children are a nuisance and a risk. On the other hand, the children see the police as their biggest enemy or threat. They are afraid of the rough treatment they get from policemen even when they are not in any way infringing the law. Hence it requires a major change of attitude for police personnel to see that these children need help. Currently, it has not been mandated for these forces to protect such children as victims on the station. If their involvement in child protection is prescribed, it can bring a significant improvement in the situation. In spite of this, Sathi has successfully persuaded them to assist in its work in most stations.

As described in Chapter 4, Sathi has been regularly recognising the support from these stakeholders. The police and railway personnel have also been invited to visit Sathi camps so that they can see what happens to the children whom they entrust to Sathi. In general, the Sathi platform staff maintain regular contact with the railway staff and the police.

Ten-year-old Golu, son of a sub-inspector, belonged to a rich and well–to-do family. The child had three brothers and one sister. All of them were going to school. Golu, unfortunately, was a slow learner, unlike his siblings. His speech was delayed too. His parents started sending Golu along with his siblings to the same school. Unable to cope, Golu was teased by his peers. One day, while visiting Gorakhpur, Golu got lost. Seeing the child sitting alone on the stairs of platforms and crying, Sathi staff approached him immediately and brought him to the shelter for help. Golu's family members were very worried about the child and had started searching for him in the neighbourhood and also at their relatives' places. Luckily, they reached the RPF station at Gorakhpur and got the information that the child was safe at the Sathi shelter. Immediately, the child's father came to the shelter to receive the child. Around 10 relatives had accompanied him to the shelter. The child's father was very happy upon seeing the child. On learning about how Sathi works, he appreciated the staff and expressed deep gratitude towards the organisation. They also donated Rs 500 and sweets for the shelter children.

As a result of such efforts, in many locations the police now refer children who seem to be in distress to Sathi's staff, or to platform staff of other NGOs. Children are likely to approach less threatening people than police or railway staff when they need help. Sathi, therefore, works with vendors and porters on the platforms, and rickshaw pullers and auto-rickshaw drivers outside the stations, in order to make them aware of the issue of runaway children. Self-employed people of this type have to work hard to make a living and runaway children often compete with them, such as by carrying passengers' luggage for lower costs than the official rates set by the railway authorities. Some of them may exploit platform children, but in either case it is not usually in their interest to treat them sympathetically. In spite of this, however, Sathi staff has developed fruitful relationships with many such people, and the coverage of the stations where they work has been substantially improved. There have been instances of Sathi Staff's family helping in rescuing a lost child.

Twelve-year old Ghanashyam was in the fourth standard when he was abducted by an unknown person while returning from tuition class in September 2009. He was brought to the Raichur railway station and taken on a train to Bangalore. After boarding the train the child started crying and shouting loudly. Since that would attract attention the abductor ran away abandoning the child. One of the staff members' fathers, Mr Bheema Raya Shali, noticed the boy and took charge. He spoke to him and convinced him that he would help him find his parents and send him home. After reaching Bangalore, Mr Shali brought the boy to Sathi Shelter. The child only knew the name of the place he lived in and did not know anything else. In the meanwhile, Mr Shali went to Yadgir on some work and spotted some posters of the boy at the Yadgir railway station. He contacted Sathi with the numbers of the boy's parents and they were contacted. The father came over to Sathi shelter and took his son. He was grateful that his son was safe. He had spent close to USD 8,000 to find his lost son.

One of the most important groups through whom Sathi can reach children who are in need of assistance, and in many ways the most difficult to collaborate with, are the 'full time' platform children, who live on or near the platforms and live by begging, doing odd jobs, stealing or otherwise. These children are in a sense beyond Sathi's reach; they have become 'hardened' to living on the platforms and have found their own ways of tolerating and even enjoying the life they have chosen for themselves. Sathi has often tried but failed to persuade these children to join their camps. These children have an interest in recruiting new children to their informal gangs. They also retain some sympathy, however, for their fellow-children who have only recently arrived, or for very young or otherwise vulnerable children. They have sometimes been persuaded to act as Sathi's 'ears and eyes', and to bring 'new' children to Sathi. Sathi's platform staff do their best to cultivate trust with these long-term child residents on the stations, even when the representatives of other more official institutions prefer to ignore them or even to regard them as enemies.

Sathi organises meetings and short plays at stations to sensitise travellers and people who work on the stations to the problems of railway children, and to Sathi's efforts to help them. A recent example of such an effort is a television spot running in Bangalore city station along with all other types of advertising and public messages. The clip can be viewed at http://backhome.sathiindia.org.

Collaborations Beyond the Platform

The CWCs are in many ways Sathi's most important resource beyond the platform. Although both Sathi and these committees are focused on helping children, there are many ways in which their relationship has the potential to become dysfunctional. It typifies the fundamental differences between government and NGO 'culture' in some ways. It is to the credit of both sides that this relationship has thus far been amicable and productive.

Sathi has played an important part in building and developing the national network of CWCs. Sathi has helped CWCs to 'network' and learn from one another, by meeting them as groups and individually. Sathi in Bangalore also publishes a regular newsletter which is widely circulated among CWCs further afield, and has set up an annual 'Best CWC Award', first in Karnataka and subsequently in Mumbai. It is organising two to three-day exposure visits for new members to visit others and invites CWC members to observe and participate in its camps. It is of course difficult to ascribe responsibility for changes and improvements in the national system to the work of Sathi, but Sathi can claim with some justification to have played a significant part in helping to make the new system work effectively. Besides this generic support, Sathi has been filling in for the shortcomings in the official system by offering secretarial and administrative support to CWC they are working with closely. This might well have evolved very differently, and some of the many NGOs which also work with street and railway children have much more difficult relationships with the official system.

Collaboration with government-run children's homes, and NGO-run homes is potentially even more difficult. Every institution, irrespective of the overall system in which it operates, has a vested interest in maintaining, and when possible, increasing the scale of its activities. For any children's institution, this means institutionalising children. Sathi is thus in some sense a potential threat, because it regards institutionalisation as a second best solution, or even a failure, compared to a successful return home. Many children whom Sathi's staff contact on railway platforms need long term institutional care. Sathi needs and relies on such institutions, but it emphatically does not run any of them itself. This is not only because such homes would divert funds, management and staff time, from the 'front-line' activity of contacting children and getting them home, but also because Sathi wants at all costs to avoid any commitment to institutionalisation.

Sathi needs to work closely with government and NGO children's institutions, so that long-term care can be available for those children who need it. Surprisingly, it has proven difficult to work with NGO homes. This may be because some of them are particularly committed to maintaining or even increasing their own numbers, perhaps with a religious agenda, and also because NGOs often find it difficult to work with one another, anywhere. Sathi works particularly closely with government children's homes, which are themselves part of the government system. Sathi helps many children's homes to trace children's addresses, using its own well-proven, but often informal methods, irrespective of whether the children were originally brought to the home by Sathi or by another organisation. It completes the reunification process in the same way it uses in its own shelters and camps. Initially, it demonstrates these methods for three months and leaves it to the management of the home to continue the efforts. Thereafter, it steps in from time to time to work with those children who have not been reunited with families for more than six months despite efforts by the staff of the home. Child counsellors have been seconded to work full time with the children at government homes.

These children are often 'harder cases', in that they have spent more time away from home than the children whom Sathi itself has met at railway platforms and have been partly institutionalised. Nevertheless, the rate of success appears to be similar to that achieved through other means. Sathi conducts workshops, training and exposure programmes for the staff of government children's homes, in the hope that they will adopt Sathi's methods of making this happen.

Sathi has also run camps on the premises of these institutions. Government institutions very clearly do not provide an environment which is conducive for these camps. The 20 or 30 children who are attending a camp are temporarily separated from the official regime. They sleep, eat, work and play as a group, along with any outsiders whom Sathi has brought to the programme, but the normal routine of the institution continues around them.

It may be that the glaring contrast between the two styles of operation itself helps the children realise how much they dislike being institutionalised and thus to be more inclined to go home. Sathi has nevertheless concluded that it is worth compromising on the issue of location, and putting up with the 'hassle' and bureaucracy involved in dealing with government, in order to reach some very troubled children and generally to infiltrate its own ideas and methods into the official system. At the time of writing, Sathi had conducted four such camps, three in the Alipore home near Delhi and one in Kolar in southern Karnataka. It was not easy to persuade the management of these homes to allow Sathi to occupy a part of their premises and to take some of their children out of their normal day-to-day routine. Even when the managers agreed, their junior staff often failed to collaborate, but nevertheless the camps were satisfactorily completed.

Sathi took over one dormitory of a government children's home for its camp. Some of the children who were inmates at the home and had attended the camp thanked the Sathi organiser profusely for leaving the doors unlocked during the night. It was normal practice for the doors to be locked, to stop the children from 'escaping', but this meant that they could not use the toilets which were adjacent to the dormitory. The results were predictably degrading for the boys and disgusting for everyone else. The Sathi staff sincerely hoped that their more liberal policy would be adopted after the camp.

A total of nearly 200 children attended the four camps and within a few weeks after the end of the camp, 70 per cent of them had been successfully re-united with their families. These were mostly children who would have spent the remainder of their childhood in institutional care. This is perhaps the best example of Sathi's collaboration with the government. Several government homes have also allowed some of their children to attend Sathi's independent camps. Sathi hopes that more homes will follow and that sending children to Sathi's independent camps will become an accepted part of their operating routines.

Partnerships with NGOs

The NGO community is of course the other main player in the field and many NGOs are less biased towards family reunion than Sathi is, for many different reasons. Sathi collaborates with over 100 NGOs, in a variety of ways. NGOs such as the Don Bosco institutions in a number of cities can often provide more suitable medium-term accommodation than government homes for children who cannot be reunited with their families.

Local NGOs can also help Sathi to trace children's home addresses, and generally to facilitate the process of getting children home in places where Sathi itself has no permanent staff. As they do this, the staff of these NGOs observe, understand and

Figure 8.1:
In a Children's Home—Drawing by a Group of Boys at a Sathi Camp

sometimes adopt Sathi's methods. Such successes cannot easily be documented and may not even be known to Sathi, but if the overall objective is achieved this is adequate return for Sathi. A number of NGOs have also collaborated in Sathi's camps. They have provided places where the camps can be held, their staff have helped to run the camps, and they have sent 'their' children to them. More generally, Sathi shares its experience and its beliefs with other NGOs and the wider community by conducting joint studies, supporting research, training, sharing staff and other forms of 'networking'.

Rahmat and Yusuf were spotted together at Lucknow railway station. They were drenched in rain. Also, they had injuries on their bodies. They were initially approached by a staff member from Ehsaas, a local NGO working on the platform. But the children refused to go with them. Ehsaas contacted Sathi and the staff met the children. They took them to a restaurant and bought them food. They then wandered around the platform with these children for about an hour. They were from West Bengal and their parents had sent them to work in a bread factory. The children were branded by a hot iron rod by their employer. Hence, they decided to run away and landed at the Bangalore station. The staff convinced the children to come to the shelter and that it would be better than being on the platform.

As a result of all this, more children have been reached and have gone home, information and experience and manpower have been shared, and the Sathi 'message' has been spread more widely.

If a for-profit business wants to extend its market, one way is to 'franchise' other entrepreneurs to use the same brand and operating methods for their own businesses, and to charge them a substantial fee for the service. Companies like McDonalds and Starbucks which may have over 30,000 franchisees, reap the benefits of their proven business methods, and at the same time avoid many of the problems of massive growth.

Not-for-profit organisations such as Sathi, which want to extend their work, but which are constrained by a shortage of money, staff or perhaps of management capacity, can adopt the same approach. In theory, if their methods are effective and their aims are shared by others, this should be an ideal way for NGOs to extend their work. In fact, however, franchising appears to be more difficult for NGOs than for businesses. The founders of NGOs are more complicated than business entrepreneurs. They want to 'do good' and tend to be passionate believers in their own ways of doing things. This passion is what enables them to start and build successful institutions, but it also inhibits their willingness to accept other people's methods completely. Social entrepreneurs may not seek financial rewards, but, like most people, they enjoy recognition and a franchising model leaves little room for that.

Sathi has nevertheless attempted to work through 23 partner NGOs in nine states, in an effort to extend its services to larger numbers of runaway children and their families. Sathi has generally adopted the following strategy in order to recruit 'franchisees' of this kind. After identifying a suitable NGO which is already working with homeless children on the streets or railway platforms, Sathi involves them in carrying out a survey of children who arrive at the main railway station in the NGO's area of operation. When the local institution is thus made aware of the scale of the problem, and of the advantages of early contact and rapid turn-around in most cases, they can be 'sold' the idea of full collaboration. Sathi then attaches one of its own staff to the potential partner for between six and 12 months. This person trains the local staff 'on the job', by demonstrating how to approach runaway children, to get their trust, and then to find where they come from and to liaise with their families to get them home. The potential partner then decides whether to carry on or not. In general, these initiatives have not been successful. Tensions have developed between Sathi and its partners, who have often resented the impression that Sathi has come to 'teach' them and is intruding on 'their' territory. Very often, the field staff are convinced and they wish to adopt Sathi's methods, but their management is less willing.

In Andhra Pradesh this process was formalised; six smaller local institutions which work for children on the stations across the state meet regularly to share information about specific cases, to avoid duplication and to aggregate information in order to reach the best solutions for particular children. Sathi was supported as an adviser by ActionAid, a UK-based international NGO which works with a variety of collaborators to put an end to poverty. The staff of the networked institutions worked closely together on the same activities, costs were shared and it was a genuine partnership. After some time, however, the collaboration failed because the responsibilities of each party had not been clearly defined from the outset and inter-institutional communication broke down. Results were not consistently documented and the partner did not follow Sathi's management information systems and case study collection procedures.

In other examples, there were fundamental differences of opinion on the issue of home placement. The Hyderabad Council of Human Welfare, for instance, agreed that family reunion was desirable, but they felt that runaway children should receive some schooling or vocational training before being sent home, in order to enable them to settle down and find a future for themselves.

Ashray of Hyderabad agreed that home is the best place for the child, and they collaborated with Sathi to achieve thus. Their success rate, however, was substantially lower than that achieved by Sathi itself. Only 60 per cent of children could be successfully sent home. A further 20 per cent went home but ran away again and the remainder had to be referred to other institutions.

Sathi also collaborated for 18 months with its namesake Saathi (with a double 'a') in Mumbai, but this involved sharing staff, methods and finance rather than a one-way transfer of the single 'a' Sathi's methods to its double 'a' partner; both institutions learned from the relationship, but it lasted less than two years. The parting was amicable, but Saathi continues to operate in Mumbai as it had before. Mumbai is of course one of the world's largest cities, and is a far greater magnet for children and all other types of migrants than Bangalore or the other smaller cities where Sathi had developed and refined its methodologies. Nevertheless, there are no fundamental differences between Mumbai and any other large city from the point of view of children who end up there, or the reasons why they have left their homes, and it is unfortunate that the thousands of children, who run away to Mumbai every year, and their families, are not benefiting from Sathi's approach.

Ehsaas, meaning 'realisation', is a small institution based in Lucknow which shares many of Sathi's values. They sent a total of 155 children home in 2010, but these were less than half the total number of children for whom they worked. They have collaborated successfully with the railway police and other authorities to create what they call 'child-friendly railway stations', and Lucknow station is as a result probably the safest station in India for a child to come to. They wanted to collaborate with Sathi in order to share their expertise in getting children home, but they felt that a broader approach was necessary; they felt that Sathi's over-riding emphasis on family reunion lead to neglect of other issues, such as the condition of children who remained on the platforms, or could not for whatever reason go home. Being a much smaller institution, dealing with a few hundred children

---

Box 8.4: *Child-Friendly Railway Stations*

A dedicated group of individuals from the Northern Railways (NR), the Railway Protection Force (RPF), the Government Railway Police (GRP), civil society organisations, citizens and children, are striving to make Charbagh in Lucknow India's first Child Friendly Station (CFS). An estimate that at least 15–20 new children arrive unaccompanied at the station every month triggered off a series of activities at Charbagh, aimed at reducing the risks faced by such unattended children at the platform.'

The police reach out to children and refer them to NGOs. They maintain a record of children they contact. The child protection booth at the station is very active and is manned by the GRP and RPF personnel. Juvenile Welfare officers are trained in child rights and they work effectively with the children. Medical care is available on the platform. Sale of drugs, prostitution and begging are curbed effectively. Banners and posters are put up on the platforms to create awareness among the public about children who run away from home. All these initiatives are supported by the Railways.

Source: Singh Shachi. 2012.

every year rather than several thousand, they feel that each case needs more individual treatment, analysis and follow-up. Ehsaas and Sathi remain on good terms, and they admire each other's work, but they do not collaborate directly.

Sathi collaborated closely with Salam Balak Trust at Old Delhi railway station for 18 months between 2005 and 2007, but the relationship did not last. They shared staff in order to provide daily coverage of the platforms and Sathi helped the Trust to organise camps, to get children home and to raise finance. This helped both institutions to reach more children than either could have done on its own. Sathi conducted a number of camps for children whom the Trust had identified on the station platforms, and the skills and capacities of the two institutions seemed to fit very well together.

The collaboration eventually floundered, however, because the basic ideologies of the two institutions were fundamentally different. Salam Balak believes strongly that they should provide a long-term tailor-made solution for each child, focused on helping him to determine his own future, even if this means that the numbers they can reach were limited. Sathi has a definite agenda and target; it wants to get as many children as possible to return home and to remain there. Salam Balak focuses more on each individual child's preferences, even if this is to remain on the platform. Like Ehsaas in Lucknow, they also want to provide assistance to children who do not want to leave the station.

Yet collaboration was with Bal Prafulta, a children's institution which works at two of the main railway stations in Mumbai, which also runs a computerised system to trace missing children. They have a similar approach to Sathi and in 2010 they successfully sent home 222 children out of the 484 whom they had contacted on the streets or in one or the two stations. Here again, the two institutions differed as to the main emphasis of their work. Sathi aimed to maximise numbers sent home, and at the same time to try to limit the numbers who ran away again. Bal Prafulta took a more cautious and personal approach and as the above figures show this meant that less than half of the children they contacted were sent home. Once children have returned home,

Bal Prafulta devotes substantial resources to trying to keep them there. Sathi, on the other hand, accepts that a small number will run away again, and prefers to focus on helping more children to go home. This reflects their belief that home is best.

Sathi's management were concerned to improve the success rate of its partnership with other NGOs, and they commissioned a small study of 14 institutions with which Sathi had collaborated. The collaborations had lasted between six months and three years. Sathi placed one of its own staff members with each partner, at Sathi's expense for the duration of the partnership and one sadly obvious result of this was that in every case the family reunion numbers achieved by the partner dropped steeply as soon as the partnership came to an end. The partner institutions were generally very satisfied with the family reunion results which were achieved during the partnership, although they felt that Sathi should have provided more funds to support the effort. They also felt that Sathi did not spend sufficient time with each child. This was perhaps to be expected, since Sathi believes very strongly that runaway children are in some sense a 'perishable' product; the longer they are away from home, the more difficult it is likely to be to get them to go back home. Sathi's ideal case, apart from a child that does not run away at all, is one who is identified by Sathi as soon as he reaches a railway platform, and is immediately assisted to go home again.

As a result of this generally unsatisfactory experience, Sathi now prefers less formal forms of collaboration, which are more for sharing knowledge than for actual joint activities. Sathi can provide training to the staff of other institutions, but actual working together 'in the field' or on the platform has generally not been a success. There are many reasons for this, including the particular nature of NGO leaders' motivation to which we have referred above, and the unusually business-like results-oriented approach of Sathi. This is not to the taste of many NGOs, some of whose leaders are in some sense refugees from the corporate sector, or have deliberately chosen a career in social service, with a master's degree in social work, rather than an MBA.

The Argument for Restoring to Family

Sathi through these partnerships has built a deep understanding about the various arguments in favour of reunion with families and the shades and nuances of other's views. Sathi strongly supports this as the best option, unless there are very strong reasons to do otherwise. Here are some of the reasons cited by Sathi and like minded people as to why a child should go home.

The 'official' view, as enunciated in the UNICEF declaration of the rights of the child, and in the relevant national laws in India and elsewhere, is that home is right. The officials who draft such documents are rarely the same people, who have to implement them, but this view probably reflects public opinion in general; children should be at home.

Clearly there cannot be any universal rule: the decision must depend on the alternative; if a child cannot return home, where should he go? In India, because fostering is in its infancy, and adoption very complicated procedurally, a children's residential institution is usually the only option, and many if not most such places are not good homes in the fullest sense. Even a brief visit to such a place is enough to show that they are not a 'home'.

Staff are the key to this issue, not money, and it has proved very difficult in India to find staff who have the necessary emotional as well as skill-based qualifications. SOS Children's Homes, for instance, have successfully developed 'artificial' homes, with nine or 10 children accommodated in one dwelling, and one house-mother or similar person to take care of them. This concept has generally not taken off in India, partly because it proved so difficult to find suitable staff and because those in the 'system' who are responsible for deciding where children should go could not easily accept the concept.

Institutionalisation tends also all too often to be a one-way street; the decision is made, and the child remains in the institution until he escapes, or grows up. Institutional children's homes may make a runaway child less able to fit back into the home from which he has run away.

Finally, and perhaps least importantly, there is a powerful cost argument. We tend to ignore cost when dealing with so fragile and emotional an issue as children's welfare, and India has vast under-spent government budgets. If the better option is also less expensive it should surely be considered. The annual cost of accommodating a child in a government children's home is much higher than the costs of NGOs and families. Thus it may be cheaper and effective if families are given some money to care for their own.

Sathi's view, based on 20 years of experience, is that a child's family and home offer the best care and protection. Despite poverty and hardship, families offer care and protection that is better than anything that can be organized by outsiders. It is not necessarily bad for children over 14 years of age to be employed if they are not inclined to continue in school, especially when their family situation requires this.

The Argument for Institutional Care

If this truth is so self evident, it is only in the relatively much smaller number of cases when the child's family is broken or dysfunctional, a suitable institution must be identified to match the child's needs. Sathi too acknowledges that there are a few instances when a runaway child should not be sent back home, and why even a mediocre institution may be better than a bad home. These underlie the general preference for institutionalisation which still applies in India.

Some children effectively have no home, or parents, because they are totally lost and their families cannot be traced. Sathi too recognises that is possible.

Poverty plays some part in most children's decisions to run away from home, and can be a reason for them not to return. Some children want to earn money and may therefore run away from school to work. Or, other children may want to study, but their families insist on making them work instead. Either way, running away seems to be a solution, or family poverty is a major cause. One option therefore, is to remove the child from the home, or to accept the child's own decision to remove himself, and to provide him with better conditions than his family could afford. This is not always possible, however. The combination of the child's own wishes, his family's need and the pressures of economic and social realities sometimes mean that it is better to accept the sad status quo and to focus institutional time and money on 'easier' cases.

A 13-year-old boy in Mumbai works as a pimp for his mother; she charges each client around fifty rupees, and earns enough to keep her son but also gives him Rs 500 a month for his own savings account. He does not go to school, and when he is older, plans to use his savings to start a business of some sort. He was picked up by the police when they raided the red light district, and handed over to a church-based children's home. He hated the home, and said that his mother needed him to maintain her business. He ran away repeatedly; the staff at the home eventually gave up trying to keep him with them.

Another 12-year-old boy had been 'sold' by his parents for Rs 5,000 to a zari embroidery workshop in Mumbai, where he had been forced to work long hours in bad light which had damaged his eyesight. He was, however, properly fed. He was seized by the police when they raided the workshop in a drive against child labour, and brought to the same children's home. He disliked being in the home and ran back to his parents' home in the slums. The owner of the zari workshop had already complained to the child's parents and he demanded that they should refund his Rs 5,000; in the meantime, he took away a neighbour's child to replace the boy. He had bribed the police to avoided prosecution for employing under-age children. The home staff concluded that it was probably best to let him go.

It is not difficult to ensure that institutionalised children get decent shelter, enough to eat, adequate medical care, be sent to school and be protected or prevented from being employed in hazardous or any other forms of work. These easily measurable indicators of well-being can be provided more verifiably and perhaps less expensively, than if the child remains in a poverty-stricken home. Loving care is less measurable and harder to provide, but many families find it hard to provide anyway and institutional care may sometimes be a better option.

If a child is sent back to the family and the outcome is bad, such as abuse or destitution, the person or official committee who made the decision can be publicly pilloried. If the same child had been sent to an officially approved institution, the decision makers could not be blamed. We live in a time of risk-aversion, which rewards the 'safe' decision.

The 2006 amendment to the Juvenile Justice Act also widens the scope of the definition 'in need of care and protection', so that it goes beyond destitution and physical harm, to include psychological harm and other less objectively verifiable criteria. This makes it easier to decide that a child should not be sent home.

The decision to institutionalise also avoids the lengthy and delicate processes of investigation and counselling, with both children and with their parents, which has to precede the actual repatriation of the child.

The 2010 Right to Education Act also strengthens the case for institutionalisation. If a child's family are unlikely to send him to school, or if there is no school available, he will be effectively deprived of his right under this Act; it can be argued that it is better to protect him from this by sending him to an institution where he is sure to get an education.

Many government homes are not full, because of over-provision, and because of competition from non-government homes, which may be of higher quality. This means that it will generally be possible to find a place for a child; the decision to institutionalise him will be implemented easily, whereas it may be difficult if not impossible to send him home.

All these are very powerful arguments, and all too often their combined impact is that the decision 'send child X to institution A' is a great deal easier to make, and to implement, than 'find out where child Y's home is, why he ran away from home, how the problems that led him to run away can be ameliorated and then decide'. This is of course particularly true if the decision-maker also runs an institutional children's home which needs to be fully occupied.

The Focus in Future

In the longer term, the government in India at the state and national levels will doubtless take on more responsibility for dealing with runaway children; they are a sadly universal problem, like sickness or crime, and should thus be dealt with by the state. Sathi is thus probably correct to focus its collaborative efforts on government institutions, such as children's homes and CWCs, difficult though this may be, because they will eventually determine the shape of India's policies and practices for dealing with runaway children. NGOs may at first sight appear more accessible and amenable to change, and the government may seem rigid and impenetrable, but Sathi's small initial successes in infiltrating the official machinery shows that this can be done, and that it will have far more substantial and longer-lasting impact in the years to come.

References

Seema. 2006. 'A Report of Collaboration and Networking with Sathi'. Report submitted by Seema, 2006 as part of course in Post graduate Diploma in Hospital and Health Management 2004–2006, Institute of Health Management Research, Jaipur 2006.

November 2011. Author's interview at SOS Children's Village.

Singh Shachi. 2012. Creating Country's First Child Friendly Railway Station, Concept and Journey. http://wcd.nic.in/icpsmon/pdf/Regional%20consultation/Child%20Friendly%20Railway%20Station%0.pdf, Lucknow, accessed on 29-07-2013.

Railway Children. 2010. 'Envisioning Our Future—Making India a Child Friendly Nation', shared with author during an interview with Railway Children India (document available with me).

Chapter Nine

Who Really Knows a Child's Need?

Children's Participation—Precept and Practice

Sathi's work is based on the premise that home is best—not every home and for every child, always, but for most children from most homes most of the time. Every individual in every organisation which works for children presumably believes the same; the difference is one of degree, how bad must a family be for it to be better for the child's decision to run away to be respected, and the child to be allowed to stay away?

Sathi's work usually involves an infringement of a child's liberty. Some children regret running away soon after they have done so, and they assist Sathi in the process of getting them home as soon as they meet the outreach worker on the platform. These are a minority, however. Most runaways do not want to go home; they believe that they were right to leave, because of what was happening to them at home, or, perhaps more often, regardless of their original reason for leaving, because they are frightened of being punished for having run away if they do go home, so they prefer to stay away.

The story as thus far related has focused very much on the various techniques which Sathi uses to get children home. Sathi's staff try to avoid losing contact even with these 'failed' cases, and they continue to make efforts to get them home even when they are officially under the care of the appropriate CWC and in a government or NGO home.

Nearly all these techniques, however, involve an element of persuasion, which necessarily requires Sathi's staff to get the children to do something that they do not want to do. There is always a delicate line, however, between compulsion and persuasion. There is much talk of 'participation' in every aspect of social work and education; the debate about children's rights is also part of the same discourse; to what extent should children themselves play a part in deciding their own future?

Roger Hart conceptualised what has become widely known as the ladder of children's participation, in order to assist children's welfare policy makers and practitioners to place their own views and practices on a continuum from minimal to maximum participation. The eight rungs on this ladder can briefly be summarised as below:

1. Manipulation of children: Effectively this is compulsion, or inducing cooperation by short term offers of food or comfort. The ladder does not include force, which is not participation at all, but this first rung is characterised as being only one stage better than overt use of force.
2. Decoration with children: Children are paraded and encouraged to appear 'on the stage' or in the meetings where their future is decided, but their views are effectively ignored.
3. Token children: A few suitably compliant children are asked to express their views, but the important decisions are made by adults.
4. Informing children: Children are told what is happening, and the reasons are explained to them; but their views on the critical issues are mainly ignored.
5. Consultation with children: Children's views on some decisions or parts of decisions are requested, and considered, and are sometimes followed.
6. Equality with children: Children and adults actually share the decision-making process, on an equal footing.
7. Driven by children: Children actually lead the process of decision making and implementation, but heavily supported and when necessary guided by adults.

8. Equity with children: Children are in charge of the whole
    process, and they actually implement all the steps of which
    they are capable. Adults are only involved when necessary,
    and with the agreement of the children.

Hart himself believed that the first three rungs were essentially
'non-participative', and the ladder is clearly intended to repre-
sent climbing up and away from methods which are not so good
towards something better; the higher rungs are preferable to the

Figure 9.1:
The Participation Ladder

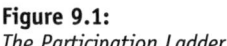

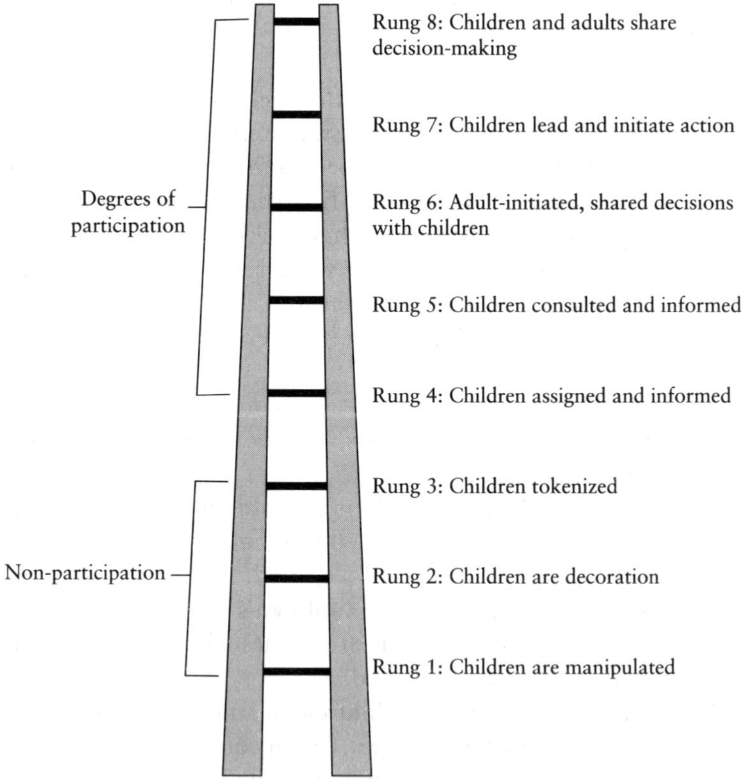

Rung 8: Children and adults share
decision-making

Rung 7: Children lead and initiate action

Degrees of
participation

Rung 6: Adult-initiated, shared decisions
with children

Rung 5: Children consulted and informed

Rung 4: Children assigned and informed

Rung 3: Children tokenized

Non-participation

Rung 2: Children are decoration

Rung 1: Children are manipulated

Source: UNICEF Innocenti Research Centre. Adapted from Hart, R. 1992. Children's
Participation: From Tokenism to Citizenship. Florence: UNICEF Innocent Research
Centre.

lower ones, and institutions which work with children should aim to move towards the eighth rung. The ladder is intended as a tool for all forms of child-related work, including ordinary classroom methods as well as what happens in correctional establishments, and the implication is that any type of interaction will be fairer, and more effective, if it is closer to the higher rather than the lower rungs. For the sake of completeness, it may be useful to add a bottom rung, number zero, below 'manipulation', which can be labelled 'coercion'; this of course involves no participation at all, except in a very limited sense, but many children's experience with the police, and then with government children's homes, cannot be labelled participative in any useful way.

From Manipulation to Equality

If we try to use this framework to assess Sathi's work we get mixed results. As we have noted above, the initial contact is necessarily almost always manipulative; a child who has just arrived at a station platform may be bewildered, uncertain and frightened, but he is unlikely to want to return home. Can we say that the Sathi process from that point onwards also progresses up Hart's ladder, so that it reaches 'equity' when the child finally goes home, and stays there? This question of course begs the question as to where on the ladder a given family's treatment of a child may lie, and Sathi does attempt to ensure that runaway children's families recognise and change any practices which may have sparked their child's urge to run away, and may cause him to run away again. But, as far as Sathi's activities themselves are concerned, it would appear reasonable to place the final act of return as being on the seventh or eighth rung; Sathi itself withdraws at this point, apart from maintaining a limited monitoring role, and the child himself is as much in charge of his own destiny as he was when he ran away; it is to be hoped that he now wants to remain at home, not to leave.

Sathi's process broadly consists of four stages; the initial contact, Sathi's own short-term homes, the camp, and the return home. If the first stage is unashamedly manipulative, as it has to be, can the second stage, a child's stay in Sathi's own short-term home, be considered as using children's nominal participation as 'decoration' or 'tokenism' or at best informing children about the dangers of platform life and the benefits of a family?

Sathi's shelters are open; the children can leave whenever they want, but they are usually sufficiently attracted by the comfort, the security, the food, the television, the games and one would hope by the engaging non-conditional affection and respect which they receive from the staff. Their preference for this over the unknown life on the platform is natural, but these children are not fools; they almost certainly realise that even a short-term open shelter can be the first step back to their home from which they have so recently fled. Many of the children have already at this point made a tacit but very important decision; they have chosen Sathi in preference to what may be the more immediately enticing possibility of joining the children who live more or less permanently on the railway station where they had once arrived. Sathi's work at this stage and in camps ranges between consultation and equality.

Platform Regulars and the Participation Ladder

Hart's ladder can equally well be applied to the process by which the children from platform gangs attract and then retain new recruits to their numbers. They manipulate them by offers of immediate gratification—food, tobacco and above all the company of their peers, one or two recently joined gang members may 'decorate' the attraction of the gang by telling them how bad the police and other 'official' alternatives are; they let them gradually into their secrets by informing them about what the gang does and then consulting with them on small gang decisions. Thus the interactions between the new arrivals and the existing gang members rapidly move up the ladder of participation until a 'new kid' attains full and genuine equity—he is himself a fully accepted member of the gang.

Sathi and other child care agencies must compete with this 'ladder'. Their staff are adults, and their aims are fundamentally based on their conviction that they know what is best for the children, and bound to be less participative, particularly in the early stages. In about four out of five cases, however, Sathi successfully 'climbs' the complete ladder, so that the child regains his sense of who he is, of his membership into his natural family, rather than of a platform or street gang or of some similar informal set of relationships within an institution.

There are, however, other 'ladders' in addition to Sathi's, and the platform gangs' informal but powerful recruitment processes. Some are shorter than Sathi's, and less costly, others may take much longer and cost much more. Sathi's staff are deeply convinced that they are right in their belief that home is best for the great majority of cases, and they believe that Sathi's quantitative results which have been so painstakingly collected and analysed bear out their conviction. They are also aware, however, that success in an endeavour of this kind, what may or may not be 'the best' approach, cannot wholly be determined by figures. There has to be an element of emotion, and of qualitative judgement. We shall therefore briefly examine a sample of quite different approaches to runaway children leaving our readers to reflect on the range of possibilities.

Alternative Views on Deeper Participation

There is a very different school of thought and practice based on participation in the fullest sense, rooted in deep beliefs about children's rights, and in the conviction that almost any human being's wishes should be given paramount importance in decisions about his or her future. Children's welfare agencies operating from this stand point focus on mitigating the dangers and hardships of the streets and platforms. They believe that railway and platform children should be able to follow their way they have chosen to live in safety and dignity. Forcing these children to go back to their families or to institutions violates their basic rights. The alleged superiority of being brought up at home is a middle class construct, imposed on children because it is the accepted practice, not because it has better outcomes. In the Indian context, they adduce the wide prevalence of child labour and exploitation within the family, which, as we have seen, is often an important reason for children running away.

It can also be argued that the scale and apparent intractability of the problem makes this 'laissez faire' approach the only one which has any chance of making a real impact on the lives of the millions of children who have chosen to leave their homes. The alternative is to 'rescue' a small number and to leave the majority to suffer; might it not be preferable to mitigate the suffering for a far larger number?

Praajak's Muktangan Shelters

This is not only a theoretical view. Praajak, a Kolkata-based NGO, has been running a programme in collaboration with the railway police called Muktangan, or 'open courtyard', since 2003. It is as yet on a quite modest scale, operating on about seven railway stations, all in West Bengal. By 2010, the programme had assisted around 1,800 children. Of these, 240 were returned to their homes and 150 were sent to residential institutions. The majority, just over 1,400 remained on the platforms, or have gone their own way to other stations, to the streets or wherever they may have chosen to go. But, they were assisted by Muktangan.

Muktangan sets up drop-in centres near the stations, where the children can have a meal, take a bath, listen to some music, play some games or learn to read, write and figure. Mountain treks are sometimes organised, and the children also perform street style theatre on the platforms to entertain passengers, and to raise awareness as well as funds. The children also help to manage the centres. They calculate how much food is needed and how much it will cost. The staff find that many of them are already adept at financial calculations because they are used to helping vendors, or to sharing out the money that they have. Many can already read and write in English and Bengali because they are used to recognising signboards on railway stations and on trains. One child was asked why he had enjoyed a week-long trek in the hills. He said that it had given him more confidence and ability to work together with his friends in their daily life at the railway station. This epitomizes the aim of Muktangan. It is not to take children away from the platform, but to enable them to have a better life on the platform. This is rather similar to the Sathi shelter in Raichur in 1993.

The children who use these centres continue to circulate in the railway system, but they have told the Railway Police and Muktangan staff that they always like to come back to stations where there is a Muktangan centre, because it makes platform life so much easier. This, in itself, shows that Praajak has revolutionised the attitudes of the railway police to platform children. In most places, the police regard children as a nuisance, and they may only collaborate with child care agencies because they know that the agencies will reduce the numbers of children on 'their' platforms. By supporting and assisting Muktangan, they are making their platforms more attractive to children, but they are still willing to do this.

The Muktangan programme is in some sense at the highest rung of the participation ladder throughout. There is never any attempt to persuade or manipulate the children into doing what they do not want to do. They can come and go from the drop-in centres as and when they wish, they can participate in whatever activities they like, they can decide to board a train and go to another station if they feel so inclined, and no attempt is made to stop them from using drugs or sniffing solution. They can if they wish attend classes where the dangers of such practices are explained to them, but it is up to them whether to follow the advice or not.

Butterflies and Empowerment of Street Children

Butterflies attempts to mitigate the hardships of children on the street or platform and enables children to acquire skills with which they can do better in future. They run 12-day centres cum street schools in Delhi, and three night shelters usually located close to the main markets, and railway and bus stations. They offer basic education as well as health care and life skills training. Their innovative 'child bank', owned and managed by the children themselves, helps children understand money, calculations and the importance of saving. Some children take tiny loans from the bank and use them to finance their livelihoods and learn the basics of financing an enterprise through this.

Butterflies staff have found that children who are working, either for themselves or for others, are less likely to become addicted to tobacco or paint thinners or other drugs. These habits cost money, but addicted children tend to finance them from begging or stealing; more legitimate earnings seem to be used for more legitimate purposes.

Butterflies also aims to climb higher on the participation ladder by involving the children in the management of their centres. This goes beyond day to day administration; the children are encouraged to join the local *bal sabha* or children's council, which advises Butterflies on policy issues.

Butterflies staff help children to go home when the child wishes to, but this is not their main focus and the proportion of 'their' children who go home is far lower than Sathi's. Butterflies believes that more that 70 per cent of the children working on Delhi's streets are there with the knowledge of the family and that the family depends on the child's earnings. It is possible that Butterflies and others like them are actually working with a slightly different segment of children who have a different requirement compared to those whom Sathi contacts. Sathi's contacts are 'fresh' and may quite quickly regret running away from home and be happy to return; Butterflies works with 'harder cases', where the family is in the background and the children do not want to lose their freedom. Butterflies aims to be non-judgemental and to assist children to make the best of whatever kind of life they want to live—be it on the street or on the railway platforms.

Advocates of this approach might infer that children who yield to well-meaning external pressures to return are 'forced' to return home, Sathi staff themselves say that 'rescued' children who run away from their short term shelters have 'escaped'. Is the anxiety to 'rescue' such children based on a misplaced prejudice in favour of what we know, and our vague fears and perceptions of what is 'correct'? It is important not to jump to conclusions. Might some of them be happier, more fulfilled, more likely to become useful members of society, if they had remained 'free' on the platform, or, if they had been sent to a decent children's institution, or to good foster parents?

Don Bosco Institutions for Youth at Risk

There are others who argue that it is too easy to criticise institutional care by pointing to the worst cases, of which India has so many, and that a good institution may be a better place for a child to grow up than many of the family homes which Sathi claims are 'best'. Even a very good home is not necessarily better than an institution for a child. The Israeli *kibbutzin* experience, where children were accommodated separately from their parents even as babies is still regarded as a success. The British public boarding schools are still the first choice of many of the elite in the UK and have been widely imitated elsewhere, including in India. The physical conditions, food and facilities in some government children's homes in India are not very different from those in these so-called 'public schools', which are actually very private indeed with annual fees of two million Indian rupees per child. (US$ 40,000 per annum)

The Catholic Don Bosco organisation has pioneered in offering a large variety of services to children through its Youth at Risk or 'YaR' network. They have about 70 centres throughout India, mainly in the south. But they also have some centres in the northeast and in Delhi. Their outreach staff work at bus and railway stations, to 'befriend and rehabilitate' homeless children. They run drop-in centres, short-term shelters, street and tent schools, libraries, medical clinics, vocational and other services. They also have a large number of schools which provide long term residential care and education, which accommodate children who have been 'rescued' from the street, railway platforms or elsewhere. They collaborate closely with the Child Welfare Committees (CWCs), by serving on the committees themselves and by helping with the membership selection process. They also run some small-scale children's homes which accommodate about a dozen children, and they have initiated some foster parenting arrangements in collaboration with their local parishioners and others. The staff of the Don Bosco schools work closely with NGOs like Sathi, the 'Childline' phone-in service, with the police and government institutions, and they are centrally involved in the development of a nationwide internet-based 'missing children's bureau'. Don Bosco's main emphasis is on the provision of care to children who are not at home, rather than on helping them to return home. Some of the children in their care do return home, and the institution follows up some of these in order to try to address their problems at the source.

Don Bosco does enable some of the children who long for their homes to return. Their home in Wadala in West Mumbai, for instance, which is a bright and cheerful place, with open gates, receives about eight new children every week from Don Bosco outreach and other organisations such as Sathi. About half of these go home, usually after two or three months. This contrasts with Sathi's quick turnaround and its success rate of 90 per cent.

APSA and Medium Term-Bridging Institutions

APSA, the Association for Promoting Social Action, with the acronym meaning 'unusual' in Hindi, works in Hyderabad and Bangalore, and represents another variant on the ladder of participation. Their school in Bangalore accommodates about 150 children, of whom two thirds are boys. Most of these have been working children and are in regular contact with their families, and parents are invited to visit their children at the school on the seventh of every month, in order to retain contact. For most of the children, the APSA school provides one year of good education and a clean well-ordered environment. When the children go home they join their local schools. These children do better in school and in their communities as a result of their experience of temporary institutionalisation. If some of them have nowhere to go they continue in the APSA school and complete their secondary education.

APSA outreach workers in the slums identify homeless children on the streets and persuade them to come to the school. They try to help them to return home, but only succeed in about one case in five. They have tried the Sathi camp approach, but for a shorter period, mainly for de-addiction and to improving children's motivation to remain in school. As with Don Bosco, it is not clear whether this lower success rate is because the children have been away from home for longer, or because they enjoy the institutional experience and prefer to stay, or perhaps because APSA's staff are themselves not fully convinced about the value of home.

Sathi aims to minimise the time a child spends away from home, because they have found that children over time become conditioned to the freedom of platform life, or even to institutional life, and are thus less likely to return home, and more likely to run away again if they do. The APSA and Don Bosco experiences would seem to confirm this belief.

SBT and Restoring Lost Childhood

Salaam Baalak Trust (SBT) recognises that for children with no home, life is a fast train to nowhere. It works to restore them to the world of childhood. Established in 1988 with the proceeds from the film *Salaam Bombay!* (1988), made on street children, SBT runs five 24-hour full care shelters for children (with one devoted to girl children) in Mumbai, Delhi and Bhubaneshwar.

It has five outreach contact points mostly near railway stations and a 24-hour toll-free helpline service, catering to children in distress all over India, in all looking after 5,000 children every year. SBT children, who have been trained in theatre, dance and puppetry, are giving performances all over the world. Since 2007, SBT, Delhi has been running the Salaam Baalak City Walk, New Delhi, a guided tour through Paharganj and New Delhi railway station areas. The guides are former street children from the trust. The walk aims to sensitize the public about street life, street children and Indian social problems.

SBT and Sathi have been partners and collaborated with each other on the New Delhi Railway platform recently. They have welcomed the children Sathi finds on the platform but are not convinced about reuniting these children with their families. On the participation scale they believe in working at the higher end.

Prayas and Child Protection

Prayas was founded in 1988 by a police officer to meet immediate needs of children, providing them shelter and education after a fire ravaged the North Delhi slum of Jahangirpuri. It now runs 231 centres, including 11 homes for children across the country in eight states, directly serving about 50,000 beneficiaries, marginalised children and over 11,000 youth and women. It is committed to the integrated model of development, to meet the fundamental needs of care, protection, shelter, food, clothing, health, recreation and above all, alternative education for holistic development of destitute children. Vocational training and life skill enhancement training is being imparted to older children and women. Its large shelter homes in Delhi are for children who have been orphaned, abandoned, sold into labour or subjected to physical or sexual abuse. It also operates a custodial shelter home for juveniles in conflict with the law, in cooperation with the Delhi government.

Prayas today stands committed, to make heard the voices of such children and believes that the needs and rights of children are synonymous. It is one of India's leading advocacy groups for the rights of children and has made contributions to the formulation of Indian Government policy and Law on Juvenile Justice.

It has partnered Sathi in its platform work and made its shelter near the New Delhi railway station available for Sathi's use. It does not specifically recognise the value of family reunion and has not integrated this into its work even after Sathi deputed its own staff to demonstrate it. Its approach is more assigning and informing children and at times bordering on tokenism.

The Pros and Cons of Institutions

In most countries the institutional approach has been more or less replaced by fostering, or by very small 'quasi-institutions' with no more than 10 or a dozen children in each, whose staff, and their relations to the children, are in many ways more similar to foster parents than to staff at a traditional large-scale children's home.

The orphanages in Romania in eastern Europe caused an outrage when they were 'discovered' in 1992. Children were living in dirty, inhuman and cruel conditions, and the international community rushed to improve the situation. The orphanages were reorganised, reconstructed and reformed. By 1995, however, it was realised that the problem was not one of bad orphanages; the very principle of orphanages was bad. A massive programme of 'de-institutionalisation' followed, replacing the existing orphanages with small quasi-foster homes, each accommodating 10 children or less. In 1994, there had been 100,000 children in the traditional Romanian orphanages; by the end of 2011, there were less than seven thousand, and it was agreed that all the orphanages would be closed by 2020. A similar policy is being followed in Ukraine and elsewhere in Eastern Europe, and in Rwanda and parts of Sudan in Africa.

Harsh Mander is one of the fiercest critics of the Indian Government's response to the problem of street or platform children. He sees children locked up in 'custodial, jail-like State-run institutions' or '*chillar* jails', meaning 'small change prisons', in local parlance. He argues for street-based outreach systems, to build on children's independence and resilience and vocational training to sharpen children's street based skills, such as those offered by Muktangan or Butterflies. Better still, Harsh Mander suggests, are open non-custodial homes, where children can come and go, but where it is hoped that they will stay, like the Don Bosco institutions. The ultimate solution, he says, albeit one rather unlikely to be widely replicated, is that provided by the Loreto Convent in Sealdah in Kolkata, where street children are admitted as boarding pupils in an elite day school. The premises are unoccupied for 16 hours a day so that a relatively small number of boarding children can quite easily be accommodated.

Mander does not mention the option of sending children home, because he believes this is not generally possible, or perhaps because it is not desirable. The Sathi experience, however, suggests that 80 per cent of the problem can be solved more effectively, less temporarily and much less expensively, by sending children home.

Experiences in Other Countries

There are many agencies worldwide which work with runaway children and many focus to a greater or less extent on getting children home. Juconi, an NGO in Ecuador, adopts a very different, slower and more expensive approach, which achieves similar results to those achieved by Sathi. Juconi, works with 400–500 street children a year. The bus stands in Guayaquil, Ecuador's capital city, play a similar role for homeless children to that of the railway platforms in India and Juconi's activities are focused there. Juconi has, like Sathi, systematised its methods through trial and error. The total process takes between three and five years. It starts with six months of regular contact on the streets, including games and some limited non-formal education. At first, as in India, most children are not willing to give their names or addresses, because they are frightened of being sent home. Gradually, however, children trust Juconi staff, and after a year or 18 months, the children move into Juconi's residential school. Juconi would prefer to send the children to local schools, but these schools refuse to take street children for fear that the street children will corrupt their more innocent pupils. In the meanwhile, Juconi makes contact with the child's home, and the children visit their families. Finally, between three and five years after they have first come into contact with Juconi, the children return home permanently. Juconi continues to support the children, and their families, and works with their siblings to address the issues which originally lead to their departure from home. In about four cases out of five, these children remain at home, and remain in contact with their families when they begin to work. Their model seems to move children through various stages of participation till the child is ready to make his or her own choice (equality stage).

In direct contrast to Butterflies, and Muktangan, Juconi deliberately avoids building on the skills that children have acquired while living on the streets. They believe that children need a clean break from their feral existence. Street life is a bit like being dependent on a drug; the addict's earlier life experience needs to be abandoned rather than supported.

A Comparison of Approaches

If we return to Hart's ladder of participation, we can see that the activities of most of the agencies working in the field can very approximately be located at one rung or group of rungs along the continuum from zero, coercion, to eight, equitable participation. We can also see that a high level of participation is not necessarily equated with major change or improvement to the children's lives. Very few really believe that children are as well off on the platform as they are at home, and that the choice should be completely up to each child.

We have attempted this comparative analysis to illustrate the invisible walls that come up between organisations as they try

Table 9.1:
Examples of Activities with Varied Degrees of Child Participation

Ladder Step	Examples of Services to Children					
	Platform Gangs	Sathi	Other NGOs	CWCs	Children's Homes	Families
0 **Coercion**	Threats, bullying				Confined	Beating, scolding
1 **Manipulation**	Introduction to platform thrills	Persuading to visit shelter Scholarships	Games and activities		Setting up child-spies	Emotional appeal
2 **Decoration** Child 'seen but not heard'	New recruit displayed to others		Street plays by children	Child invited to sit with CWC off	Sweets from minister	Child's achievements showcased
3 **Tokenism** pliant children used as props	Member expected to be loyal	Child's views in CWC meetings	Sharing success stories only	Few runaways met	'Good' children involved in tasks	'Good' children presented as role models
4 **Information** Child assigned and informed	How to earn a living on platform	Health risks Guidance on family	Bridge schools, vocational training	Advise on a better future	Education, vocation skills	Parents choices for school/ hostel/ vocation

5 Consultation Child consulted and informed	Ask new member about preferences	Address tracking. Guidance Counselling	Counselling, guidance, advisory services	Listing options to child for decision	Child transferred to home district	Child's preference checked for decision
6 Equality Adult-initiated, shared decision		Child agrees to go to camp	Open shelters in platforms	Child, parent given equal opportunity to talk		Child cooperates with family decisions
7 Child-driven Child=led decision or action	Children's livelihoods on platforms	Child escapes from Sathi Child's responsibilities in camp	Bal Sabhas		Child escapes from Govt Home	Child runs away
8 Equity Shared decisions	Core membership in gang	Counselling family, Reunion, Long-term settlement	Child's contribution in running shelter	Best interests of child explained		Child's choice of vocation or schooling.

Source: Authors research and analysis.

collaboration. Though the agencies may be dealing with very different groups of children their beliefs about child participation are reflected in their practices.

Muktangan, SBT and Butterflies work near the highest rung of the ladder with street children who come and go and do as they wish. They may even help to manage the agency itself, and they are presumably happier than they would be if they had not received any assistance. The many agencies which work in this way, running street schools and drop-in shelters of one kind or another, are doing good work, which is highly participative, but it is essentially a palliative and not a cure. Prayas works more at the level of assigning and informing.

Most government agencies such as the police and official residential children's homes have traditionally worked near the bottom rung, at zero or one, the level of coercion or manipulation. They ignore the problem as far as possible and this only breeds more of the same problem.

Sathi's processes, covers the whole ladder, from the initial necessarily somewhat manipulative contact on the platform which is on rung one, to a child's voluntary reunion with his family and his return home, which can only take place if the child and his parents are fully in agreement. This is because, Sathi recognises the turmoil and changing emotional state of the child and works differently with children in different emotional states. This is surely participation as it should be. Such a range of approach is necessary because of the heterogeneity of children who are out on the platform. The needs of each category of children have to be separately considered.

Sathi's work and our analysis has focused almost completely on boys who run away from home and take a train. Sathi's system is far from perfect, but it has shown that just about any child who has run away from home can be helped to return. It is not possible to achieve 100 per cent success, and not every child has a home, or should return to whatever home he does have, but most children can be got home, willingly, will stay there voluntarily, and will be better off there after this 'rescue'.

Does the Sathi approach, at or near the bottom of the participation ladder, the initial 'manipulation' on the platform, the subsequent shelter and camp process, actually amount to a subtle form of brain washing? Does this conflict with children's rights or does it work in the 'best in interests of the child'? We leave the question with the reader.

References

Hart, R. 1992. 'Children's Participation: From Tokenism to Citizenship'. Florence: UNICEF.
Kolkata Now. April–June 2011. Accessed on 26 September 2011. Maidment, David. 2011. 'Increasing Police Co-operation', retrieved from http://www.abctales.com/story/david-maidment/other-railway-children-chapter-11-extract-increasing-police-co-operation, London, accessed on 28-07-2013.
http://en.wikipedia.org/wiki/Salaam_Baalak_Trust, Wikipedia, 2012, Salam Balak Trust, http://en.wikipedia.org/wiki/Salaam_Baalak_Trusthttp://www.salaambaalaktrust.com/Vision.html. Accessed on April 2012.
http://www.salaambaalaktrust.com/Vision.html
Prayas. 2012. Retrieved from http://www.prayaschildren.org/about.html, New Delhi. Accessed on April 2012.
http://www.prayaschildren.org/about.html
Mander, H. 2011. 'Way of the Rainbow', retrieved from http://www.thehindu.com/opinion/columns/Harsh_Mander/barefoot-way-of-the-rainbow/article2597649.ece. Accessed on 3 August 2013.
The Hindu, 6 November 2011. 'Way of the Rainbow'.
De Benitez ST. 2001. 'What Works in Street Children Programmes—The Juconi Method', International Children's Federation, Baltimore 2001. Retrieved from http://www.childhope.org.uk/wcore/showdoc.asp?id=1112. Accessed on April 2012.

Chapter Ten

Care and Protection Services for Children in the UK

Kate Bulman

Children's Rights and Safety in the United Kingdom

The primary focus of this chapter will be on two groups of children in the UK; those who have been taken away from their families and placed in the care of the authorities due to concerns about their welfare at home, and those who have run away from home or the care provided by the state, whose whereabouts are unknown and who may be staying on the streets. The chapter will provide a picture of the reasons why children are taken into care or run away from home or care in the UK, and of the support and services that are offered to these children.

The UK Children's Act 2004 defines the rights of all children and safeguarding them from harm is a principle embedded in public policy. Professionals from all agencies have a duty to report information to the authorities about any child that they consider to be at risk of harm. Members of the public are also expected to report any concerns that they have relating to any child. Services provided for children have become increasingly integrated so that co-ordinated help is provided and agencies share information with one another. The term 'Parenting Capacity' has emerged over the years and refers to a parent's 'ability to provide basic care, ensure safety, emotional warmth, stimulation, guidance and boundaries and stability'. The principles enshrined in the United Nations Convention on the Rights of the Child are reflected in the 1989 and 2004 Children's Acts in the UK. A government document, 'Every Child Matters' (2003, TSO, London) outlines five outcomes which are considered key to children's well being; these are staying safe, being healthy, enjoying and achieving, making a positive contribution and achieving economic well-being. Various services are provided to all families with children in the UK to help achieve these outcomes. These include a midwife's support during pregnancy and immediately after the birth of the baby, a named health visitor for all children under five and education and support by teachers and other professionals. The great majority of families take the initiative in accessing services provided.

Children are perceived by professionals as being 'in need' when it seems unlikely that they can reach a satisfactory level of health or development without intervention. Efforts are made to help parents to access various forms of support with the aim of minimising any risks present. In more deprived areas, Children's Centres offer a range of services with this aim. When children are considered likely to suffer significant harm, compulsory intervention into family life is initiated in the best interests of the child, and in some cases the child can be compulsorily taken into the care of the social services.

Looked-After Children

The most clearly identifiable group of children not living with their birth families are 'looked after', which means that they have been taken into the care of the local authority, because they are perceived to be at serious risk of harm if they remain with their families. Substantial measures are put in place to identify families who are not coping and the number of children going into care has risen over recent years. The number of children in care in March 2010 was 89,000, out of a total population of approximately 15,000,000 under-16-year-olds. Around 70 per cent of children in care have been placed there as a result of a care order being made by the local authority because the child is at risk of suffering significant harm due to neglect, physical, sexual or emotional abuse. Around 30 per cent of children are placed into care as the result of a voluntary agreement between parents and the local authority. This arises when a child approaches the social services due to an abusive home life, or a child's behaviour is a threat to others in the home or when parents are unable to cope due to their own mental or physical illness or a child's disabilities.

Under a care order, the local authority is responsible for looking after the child, providing accommodation and ensuring that the child's welfare needs are met. A care order can only be made for children under 17 years of age (or 16 if the child is married) and can only last until a child's 18 birthday. When children are adopted they cease to be under the care of the local authority.

The situation for children looked after by local authorities has changed significantly in the last three decades. While in the past they were usually placed in large residential homes, around 75 per cent of children in care now live with foster families. This is partly due to a series of high profile abuse scandals in some large children's homes, and the recognition that children are likely to thrive better in a smaller, more family-like environment. Foster parents are families or individuals who have been approved and trained according to nationally set standards, and have foster children living with them in a spare room in their homes. Residential care still exists in the UK, but instead of large institutions, Children's Homes now only house four or five children and these are often the most difficult children. Residential care in the UK today is extremely expensive at over £100,000 per year per child, whereas the cost of foster care is considerably cheaper at around £20,000 per year per child. A young Asian woman recalls (see Box 10.1) her experience of being taken into care and put in a residential home about 15 years ago.

My first experience of care was in a residential care home. There were children of all kinds of backgrounds and I had to fit somewhere into that pattern. The staff worked in shifts and clocked in and clocked out. The face you say goodnight to is not the same face that will greet you in the morning. The office was decorated with house rules and a staff rota. I was very daunted and felt very tiny in my small frame. All I could do was cry. I wanted to go home, to be in the comfort of what I knew. I was shown around but it was just a big house that looked unfriendly. I was told names but it was just jargon to me. It was a very chaotic place. The people running it were of different races and backgrounds. You had to stand in a queue just to be fed. The food that was served was not the type I was accustomed to. Yet, as I understood it, my being here was my punishment for disclosing my problems at home to the authorities. I had to accept this. I felt uncomfortable, unsafe. I certainly did not belong there. The residents of the home did not make it easy; if I had anything of value it would be stolen or defaced. Apparently nobody likes the new person. I was shown to my room and learned that I had to share it with two other girls. I had to stop my tears. I had to learn to live life again. I wanted to talk to my family, but I was not allowed. This was yet another rule that was made on my behalf.

In time I got used to it. I had to come out of my comfort zone. I had no self esteem and very low confidence and yet I was thrown into what a felt like a cage with hungry lions ready to eat me. Slowly but surely I got used to it. I learned the tricks of the trade, how to be nice to the staff to get an extra half hour before bed, how to fake a tummy ache and get out of school. A lot of the youngsters in the home were aggressive, some of them self harmed and others were into petty crime. To be accepted and to be their friend, I had to be like they were. I started smoking and part time drinking. I truanted a lot; it made the residents respect me because I was "hard". I knew that a lot of the residents were merely acting to survive this game. There were a lot of misunderstood angry children. They found it hard to be themselves; they had to put up a barrier. They were wiser than authorities gave them credit for but if they showed their human side, they would lose. You had to put up a wall to survive, a barrier that a social worker couldn't break down, and the, social workers probably would not have had the time even to try to break it down. As long as they stuck to the protocols then that was all that mattered.

Whenever I went out, it had to be with an escort, it was very hard to walk down the street with a black or white person, just in case somebody I knew saw me. Who would I say my escort was? I had the pressure to save my family from shame; nobody must know that I was in care. If it was an Asian person, I could pretend it was a relative. Surely the social workers should understand that cultural needs should be met?

My culture is my identity, my identity is my sense of belonging and without that I am nobody. I am lost. I did however make some good friends. I noticed that trying to get one-to-one staff attention was also something that the residents, including myself craved. It was a very lonely place to be, full of people yet lonely. We were all "Kids in Care" and so often we took comfort from having this in common. Although the social services staff did not have much time for us they arranged for residential trips such as adventure holidays to build our self-respect and sense of belonging. There are a lot of positive aspects of team bonding activities like this. I learned my strengths and weaknesses and it is very important that residential care homes continue to provide such activities. I think the aspect of the residential home that I liked once I got used to the noise was the hustle and bustle, you can drown yourself and not be noticed. I like the fact that after lights went out, the other girls and I would chat long into the night and share our experiences and sneaky fags outside the barred windows.

Foster Care

Over 59,000 children live with 45,000 foster families across the UK each day, and these children amount to about four-fifths of all the children in care in Britain. Foster carers have to complete pre-approval training and are offered ongoing professional development support throughout the time that they are foster carers. There are National Minimum standards in place for foster carers which aim to ensure positive welfare, health and educational outcomes for all children and also to reduce any risks to their welfare and safety.[7] Background checks are made on the foster parents, including identity checks and criminal records checks, and personal references are taken to ensure that the prospective foster parent are suitable to work with children. Any identified failure to meet the requirements may lead to conditions being placed on a foster carer's registration. All foster carers receive an allowance to cover costs and around half also get paid a fee for their time, skills and experience. Fostering has historically been a voluntary activity in the UK, but a shortage of foster carers, particularly for more challenging children has led to the payment of fees in many cases. Though several fostering support groups campaign for fees to be paid to all foster parents, the current government has recommended that allowances will be paid to all foster parents, and fees will only be paid based on the needs of specific children. Some children live with foster families for just a few months, while others will remain with foster parents for several years. In some cases (10 per cent) children are placed with relations or family and friends foster carers, who are members of their extended family or friends. In these cases allowances are to be paid, but fees are less likely to be paid.

Foster care has the advantage of providing a home like environment for a child, and many children who have lived in foster care, even if it is not with their extended family, feel that these families in some way become their own. Many remain in touch with their foster parents throughout their lives. The account in Box 10.2 is by the same young woman who wrote about her experience of residential care in Box 10.1. When she was 13 years old, she was moved from the residential care home into foster care and remained with her foster carers until she was 16.

I remember walking into this beautiful Victorian style house. It had three floors. I was awed. This was my new foster placement. My foster parents were both of Asian origin and they had this look that showed that they were very homely people. Their smiles were genuine and not painted on but I could not smile back. I had once again walked into another unknown territory and my barriers went straight up. How could I trust them? And if I did, would I be moved again? I was asked to call them Uncle and Aunty which I was happy to do. Not only is this a form of respect for Asian elders, it also made me feel like the title itself had some meaning, a sense of belonging. The house felt so quiet that I could hear my own heartbeat. They showed me around. It was very different from the care home; the sitting room was nicely furnished with matching furniture and decor. There was no random kid sprawled out on the sofa or nobody hiding the TV remote. The bathroom smelt fresh, no queues and definitely no obscene graffiti; just the one bathroom for the family, not separate ones that said 'male' and 'female'. The kitchen smelt of home-baked bread and was not a cafeteria and the rooms were not dormitories, in fact I had my own room. I was an individual again. There were no house rules and rotas on the wall and the best thing was, the people stayed the same every day—the same Aunty and Uncle.

The first night, I could not get used to sleeping on my own. Aunty came into my room and sat with me; she held me and hugged me. I just cried. It was a very long time since I had experienced that motherly affection—even just a hug. My foster parents were great. I changed my bad habits. I did not feel the need to rebel anymore; I did not need to show my fellow residents I was 'hard'. I had chores to do on weekends, I got pocket money. Coming from a deprived home, I did not know how to accept these things. I felt guilty for allowing myself to feel gratitude. That was something I had never had before. Aunty cooked a lot of Asian traditional food. To culturally match a child is extremely important. When you remove a child from home, you have already taken away all that they know and are accustomed to and the child's culture plays a huge role in their life and that needs to be acknowledged. It gives a sort of rope to hold onto so slowly you can climb up and rebuild your life. Although I missed home, I mainly missed my siblings, and yes in a way my parents too. I did not allow myself to think of the bad things that had happened but Aunty suggested I have supervised visits and as awkward as it was, it was better than nothing. I had foster siblings, I had a home, my own room, and I finally began to feel like I belonged somewhere. I could walk down the street with my foster parents with pride and nobody would know that I was a child in care. Through there were many ups and downs, Aunty and Uncle provided me with constant support. They taught me to feel safe, to be safe. They taught that I was not to blame for the circumstances that led to me going into care. They taught me right from wrong, they gave affection without holding back and in turn I let go of my barrier, I began to form a bond and that is a bond that we took into my adulthood and is still on-going today. Having the positive influences from my foster parents, having had adequate time to build positive relationships with them, I realised that I have picked up a lot of traits that one often picks up from their own parents. This I have taken into my adult life with me and it has indeed helped me stay on track.

There is a shortage of foster carers in the UK and it is often difficult to find placements for young people that fit their needs. Too many children in care move from placement to placement, which is extremely unsettling and damaging to their life chances. Around 45 per cent of foster placements have broken down within two years. Though only 10 per cent of foster children are placed with family and friends, 72 per cent of these placements are still stable after two years. Eighty per cent foster placements in New Zealand are with family and friends. Such placements are rarer in UK because of concerns over issue of contact with birth families and such families are often in financial hardship. But it is ironical that when children are placed with family or friends, the financial and other support they need from social services is likely to be significantly less compared to being placed under foster care.

Residential Care

Around 10 per cent of children in care in the UK live in residential child care. Placements in residential care are usually made when foster placements are not considered suitable to meet a child's complex needs. Residential Child Care Homes are usually small with only four or five children living in the Home. They include short and long term placements, some providing specialist care for children with disabilities, residential special schools, therapeutic communities, adolescent psychiatric units and secure children's homes for children who have been in conflict with the law. Adults working in most types of residential care are expected to have achieved a national vocational qualification in child care and managers of homes are expected to have achieved a higher level diploma, but none are required to be educated to degree level. Staff working in residential care are expected to create a caring, healthy, stimulating, safe and secure environment for the children and young people in their care. There is usually a 'key worker' for one or more children. This person is the main link between the child's family, the social worker and their school. Residential homes are regularly inspected according to national minimum standards in a similar way that foster carers are.

Article 12 of the United Nations Convention on the Rights of the Child states that, 'When adults are making decisions that affect children, children have the right to say what they think should happen and have their opinions taken into account'. A culture of listening to children is embedded in policies relating to children in the UK. This is integral to the care system in the UK whether children are in foster care or residential care. Access to independent advocacy services in order to voice their concerns or complaints is a right of all children and young people who are looked after by social services. There are national guidelines outlining what these services should provide. However, despite this some argue that listening to and involving children in decisions that affect them does not go far enough in the UK, and that too much of a 'welfare' model exists which 'constructs a view of protection as a process determined and provided by adults for children, largely without reference to children themselves'.

Future Prospects for Children in Care

The government in the UK has invested considerable time and money in trying to improve outcomes for young people growing up in care. Though there have been some improvements, the overall outcomes for children who grow up in foster care or residential care are still poor. These children are over represented in a range of vulnerable groups. For example 35 per cent of children leaving care are not in education, employment or training at the age of 19, which compares with a national average of just over six per cent. They have fewer qualifications; they are more likely to be excluded from school and are more likely than the rest of the population to be teenage parents, young offenders, drug users and prisoners. They are also more likely to have their own children taken into care.

The UK takes considerably less children into care than do most other European countries, and only half as many as France and Denmark, but outcomes for children who are taken in to care in the UK are considerably worse than children from Denmark or Germany. For example, in Germany, children who grow up in care perform better educationally on average than do children from un-troubled families who live at home. In the UK, only six out of 100 children in care go to university, whereas in Denmark it is six out of 10. It is therefore not simply being taken into care that is leading to poor outcomes for children in the UK, but the process of being taken into care and the nature of the care itself. A recent report for Barnados, a long-established children's charity, calls for an overhaul to the care system in the UK to include earlier intervention in troubled families, minimum delay and long term stability while in care.

A UK parliamentary group has taken a particular interest in the Danish system, where outcomes for children are significantly better. Interestingly, although more young people are taken into care in Denmark than in the UK, in the majority of cases this is with the voluntary agreement of the parents (91 per cent). Reasons why young people are taken into care are broader and there is a clearer focus on the child's problems as well as the parent's problems as being a reason for entering the care system. In most cases links are retained with birth families, and entering care is in many cases perceived as form of family support in a way that it is not in the UK, where it is more likely to be seen as a last resort, when support offered has failed. In Denmark, it has been found that children in the age group between eight and 12 entering high quality residential care have lesser negative outcomes later on. Denmark uses more residential care than UK, with 41 per cent of children in residential homes and 48 per cent in foster care. A reason for the success of the care system in Denmark may also be due to a smoother process of going into care with less delays and more stability for children once they are in care. This may be easier because in Denmark most children are placed in care voluntarily and so the process is less adversarial than it is in the UK.

In early 2012 the case of the Bhattacharya family in Norway received a great deal of attention in the Indian media. Their two children were taken into care by the Norwegian state child welfare service because of perceived problems in their home environment, some of which seemed to relate more to their 'foreign-ness' than to any absolute standards of what is right or wrong for a child. As always, there were errors on both sides of the dispute, and the social worker who was responsible for the case, and who happened to be English, appears to have been unusually insensitive. The case did, however, highlight the differences between the British and the Indian approach and that in Scandinavia. Apparently over 10 times as many children are taken into care in Norway as in the UK, in relation to the population, but it must be remembered, as stated above, that in most cases the decision to take a child into care is agreed or even initiated by the parents.

Adults who work in residential homes in Europe are professionals and many have studied 'Social Pedagogy' or education for life for over three years at university. Within the social pedagogic approach to care provision for children the social pedagogue's role is to support the child's overall development, and learning, care, health and general well-being are seen as inseparable. As well as working towards ensuring earlier intervention, less delay and more stability for children in care in the UK, there is a growing interest in social pedagogy, and the approach is being piloted in 30 sites across the UK. The Essex county council in the UK is training all its staff in social pedagogy and the positive results of this for children are already being seen.

Runaway or Detached Children

Charlene's street family is a group of homeless adults, some of whom remind her that the streets are a dangerous place for a young girl. At any mention of social services, Charlene threatens to run away from the safety of her street family: from Charlene's perspective, social services failed to protect her when she was living at home being abused. Whilst Charlene, now thirteen, describes how some of her street family look out for her, protect her and share what they have with her, others encourage her to take heroin and one homeless adult has become Charlene's boyfriend.

A far less visible group of children not living with their birth parent/parents in the UK is children who have run away from home. In Britain 84,000 children run away overnight on at least one occasion each year. Of these, 55 per cent run away on one occasion, but 42 per cent run away on more than one occasion and 16 per cent say that they have spent more than four weeks away from home. These children who spend longer periods of time away from home or care are often referred to as 'detached' because they are not living at home or in care and are not accessing support from social institutions. They are instead relying on informal networks for support and while half seek support from adults in their communities such as relatives, friend's parents or neighbours, some live on the streets. As the above quotation clearly illustrates, those who provide them with some form of protection, may also be exploiting them and causing them harm. The Children's Society reports that 26 per cent of children who run away have at least one harmful or risky experience while they have been away from home. There are a few examples of good practice across the country supporting young runaways. Currently there are very few refuges in the UK and Safe@last in Yorkshire is one of these.

SAFE@LAST has 16 staff members and many volunteers. They provide a 24 hour Helpline, a Missing Young People's service,

*a Preventative education programme and, a refuge for children
and young people under the age of 16. Young people present
with many complex issues including neglect, physical abuse,
self harming, forced marriage, conflict and violence at home,
sexual exploitation and mental health problems. Since 2005
SAFE@LAST has worked with over 4,000 young people and
has made a difference to the lives of the great majority of them.
We are seeing great results from our work, and as a result our
staff and volunteers are receiving awards for their contribution
to social care in South Yorkshire and being consulted for their
expertise and knowledge in this area.*

These runaway and 'detached' children reveal the failings
not only of many children's home lives, but also of the system
intended to support them. Quite shockingly, despite there being
a considerable infrastructure in the UK to identify and support
vulnerable children, of those children who run away or become
detached in the UK, around two thirds have not been formally
identified as being 'in need' and thus requiring targeted support
from services available. As the following quote illustrates, there
are many vulnerable young people slipping through the net of
the system designed to protect them:

> Despite a range of legislative measures, guidance and policy com-
> mitments there are too many children and young people in the UK
> who do not receive the support and care they are entitled to, though
> rhetoric claims to provide for all children and young people under
> the age of 16.

The majority of children who run away are not reported to the
authorities (70 per cent). Running away is often part of a continuum of spending increasing amounts of time away from home
and on the streets. The most common reason cited for running
away from home is 'family problems'.

The Children's Society report found that there is a very strong
link between family relationships and running away. Children
who have experienced family change, such as separation of parents, a new step-parent, or the death of a parent, are three times
more likely to run away than children who have not, and they are

six times more likely to run away if they have experienced conflict within the family. Children living with both birth parents had the lowest rate of running away. Though the overall majority of children who run away had run away from home, children who are living in care are three times more likely to run away than children living with their families.

The report which contains the results of interviews with a number of 'detached children' found that generally, children who have run away from home, have fraught family lives, with parents who have issues which prevent them from having loving relationships with their children. Many live in lone parent households, many do not know the identity of or have contact with their biological fathers; many also have difficulties in their relationships with step parents. Many children had parents who were violent or took drugs and many lived in households where there was domestic abuse. The majority were from low income families and one fifth lived in poverty, though the quality of family relationships was more important than economic factors in determining whether children ran away. The children had often been neglected and emotionally abused, and many of the young people had played the role of young carer to younger siblings. Another perhaps more unusual finding was that many children cited 'secrets and lies' in family life as a having a damaging effect on family relationships. Often children knew or suspected the truth about lies that had been told to them, such as the true identity of their biological father, but did not reveal this and this was a factor in the breakdown of relationships within the family.

There are many complex reasons why so many young runaways or detached children are not availing of the support services designed to help them. It may be that problems in families have come to be seen as the norm, especially if they have been experienced for more than one generation, and that this is a factor in preventing adults and children from seeking help. It may also be that families mistrust the services which are designed to help them. It is increasingly cited that parents may not seek help with their problems for fear of their children being removed. Parents may also use the threat of being taken into care to prevent their children from seeking support:

She (Mother) used to tell me that I wasn't to tell anyone what was going on at home, about her using drugs and staying out all night and me looking after my little brother, cos we'd get put in a children's home. (Off the Radar 2009)

The plight of run away and detached children has attracted more attention over the last decade in the UK partly as a result of research into their situation. A detailed piece of research was 'Still Running' first published by the Children's Society in 1999, and has been updated twice since then, in 2005 and in 2011. Though more is now known about the issues these children face, there is little evidence that the numbers of children who run away or the risks they face have lessened over the past decade in the UK.

Various strategies have recently been put in place to support runaway children. A government report, 'Statutory guidance on children who run away and go missing from home or care, Department for schools children and families 2009', emphasises the importance of young runaways being offered a return interview when they are found or return and stresses the importance of information sharing and using a common assessment process for all children who run away. This report is currently being revised to include recommendations put forward in The Children's Society report 'Still Running 3', 2011).

Conclusion

This chapter has provided information about children at risk of harm within the home, and children who run away in the UK. The legislation and services available to children considered to be at risk within the home is well developed, though it is clear that not all children in need of help or at risk are reached. Even if they are reached, they often experience great instability in the care system and the large numbers of children who run away from home or care each year are an indication of this. Recent moves to identify and support children at risk of running away and their families or carers will hopefully have a positive impact and so reduce their likelihood of running away. Providing effective support to families that leads to genuine change is extremely difficult. Reasons for problems within families are often so complex and deep, and in the UK, families often mistrust those who intervene in their lives, especially due to the fear and stigma attached to children being taken into care. However, the key to improving outcomes for these children lies in improving life experienced within families, and in some cases in removing children from living at home in a timely way and into a stable life in the care system. Work needs to be done on changing the public perception of the care system as not being against families but being there to support families, and crucially children. The following extract written by the young Asian woman (who had grown up in care) on her life since leaving care, illustrates the difficult legacy that being removed from ones birth family and growing up in care in the UK can leave but also what ultimately can be gained from taken into care and fostered by a stable and caring family.

When I left the care system, I became lost. As much as I detested having social workers dictating my life, I could not seem to think for myself. The local authority had been my parents for so long that I suddenly felt like an orphan. I still needed their protection, their guidance and their approval. It was like the moment I became 18, I was an adult and they no longer needed to help me. They did try to rehabilitate me in an independent home but I longed to be part of a family again. My foster parents had moved away due to family needs. They assured me that I was welcome to visit and stay whenever I wanted which I did on many occasions. Although I tried to understand their reasons, I felt betrayed and neglected. I took the only direction which I could make sense of and that was returning back to my birth family home. Now an adult, I made a choice that not even the local authority could deter me from as I was no longer their responsibility. Had I made the right choice? My feelings of belonging never went away; I still needed that comfort of my own home. My parents had the power back and their first move was bribe me into a false sense of belonging where I found myself boarding a plane to my country and returning six months later as a married woman.

It wasn't a choice that I made or a choice that I even had but nevertheless it had happened and I had a role that could I play. I was a wife. Maybe it was God helping me but my husband turned out to be a good man and his family took me in and gave me a place that was rightfully mine. I stayed married because I had a new family and one that would grow to love me and nobody could take this away. I think that is why I did not try to escape my arranged marriage, it gave me a purpose. In time I set up home with my husband. The care system gave me £1,000 to help me set up my new home and my support group remained the same. My foster parents encouraged and supported me as did my good friends who had followed me through my life in care. I did not like making new friends for fear of being judged. I would most definitely agree that it was having this support network that helped me become the person that I am today. I learnt housekeeping, routine, organising and budgeting skills from my foster parents and the amazing thing is I did not like doing these things when I lived with them, but I do those things today. I now have four beautiful children. Just like my foster mother did, I teach them chores, I keep my house very tidy, I iron every Sunday and I fine my children a pound if they say bad or unkind words. I use the same sanctions and rewards as my foster mum. My siblings are very different. Whilst my home is organised and everything has its place, their homes are cluttered and chaotic as was my parents. I believe these are traits we pick up from the environment we grow up in. I am still very weary of social services and on a few occasions they have picked up on something from my past and interfered in my life. I know that this is because I have grown up in care.

Social services sometimes believe that as I did not know how to protect myself as a child I may not know how to protect my own children. They have been mistaken and then left me alone. My history of self harm has also hindered the type of medical treatment I have received in the past and each time I have had a baby social services have had to suddenly make an appearance, but I have learnt to now cooperate as I am very confident that they will find no fault, and I have been right too. *Being in care has made me strong and outspoken. I do not like social services, but I know it's their job and I love my kids too much to let them come to any harm as I know what emotional and physical harm can do to a child. I know the moves and choices I have taken throughout my life since leaving care are mostly because I have lived in care. For example, I have brought a five bedroom house in the hope that someday I too will foster and give a child a loving home. I am currently doing an access to health course with the ultimate goal of going to university and working in the nursing field. My foster mother was a nurse and my foster sister a doctor. But who knows, I may even become a social worker. I have plans to give back what the care system gave to me. Help those in need. My friends and my foster parents are still alongside me to this day and encourage me through my life. My relationship with my parents and siblings has had its moments but is still estranged. I don't think that will ever change. I am happy and content. I have a place to belong. I have goals for my future and my children give me a reason to keep going, and I give them a reason to have a happy childhood. I have a house that I have worked hard to make a home and I am never alone. I appreciate the good moments. My life in care has taught me that.*

References

Aldgate, J., H. Cleaver and I. Unell. 2011. *Children's Needs—Parenting Capacity.* TSO: London.

The author has rewritten based on the research from the site. The Fostering Network. www.fostering.net

The author has rewritten based on the research from the site. Directgov website, Children in Care, Care Orders, www.direct.gov.uk

The author has rewritten based on the research from the site. The Fostering Network. www.Fostering.net

Hacker, R. 2011. *Children in Care Statistics.* House of Commons Library.

The author has rewritten based on the research from the site. The Fostering Network, www.fostering.net

Department for Education. 2011. 'Fostering Services: National Minimum Standards'.

'Training and financial support for foster carers': www.direct.gov.uk and The Fostering Network, www.fostering.net The author has rewritten based on the research from the site.

The author has rewritten based on the research from the site. The Fostering Network, www.fostering.net

Department of Health. 2002. 'National Standards for the Provision of Children's Advocacy Services'.

Lansdown, G. 2011. 'Children's Welfare and Children's Rights' in L. O'dell and S. Leveret (eds), *Working with Children and Young People*. The Open University.

Department for Education and Skills. 2006. 'Care Matters: Transforming the Lives of Young People in Care'.

Wood, C. and L. Bazalgette. 2010. *Loco Parentis*. Demos: London.

Smeaton, E. 2010. 'Off the Radar'. Report on railway children. Railway Children.

Smeaton, Emilie (2010), Off the Radar: Children and Young People on the Streets in the UK: Executive Summary, retrieved from, http://www.basw.co.uk/resource/?id=1715 accessed on 29-07-2013.

The Children's Society. 2011. 'Still Running 3'. Report on runaways. The Children's Society.

Reports and Papers

Aldgate, J., H. Cleaver and I. Unell. 2011. Children's Needs—Parenting Capacity. TSO: London.

Hacker, R. 2011. Children in Care Statistics. House of Commons Library.

Department for Education. 2011. 'Fostering Services: National Minimum Standards'.

Department of Health. 2002. 'National Standards for the Provision of Children's Advocacy Services'.

Lansdown, G. 2011. 'Children's Welfare and Children's Rights' in L. O'dell and S. Leveret (eds), Working with Children and Young People. The Open University.

Department for Education and Skills. 2006. 'Care Matters: Transforming the Lives of Young People in Care'.

Wood, C. and L. Bazalgette. 2010. Loco Parentis. Demos: London.

Smeaton, Emilie (2010), Off the Radar: Children and Young People on the Streets in the UK: Executive Summary, retrieved from, http://www.basw.co.uk/resource/?id=1715 accessed on 29-07-2013.

The Children's Society. 2011. 'Still Running 3'. Report on runaways. The Children's Society.

Internet

The author has used information from the websites

The Fostering Network. www.fostering.net

Children in Care, Care Orders, HYPERLINK, 'http://www.direct.gov.uk', www.direct.gov.uk

Training and financial support for foster carers, HYPERLINK 'http://www.direct.gov.uk' www.direct.gov.uk

Chapter Eleven

The Future—Railway Children in the Next Twenty Years

Sathi and the National Problem

The poet Jonathan Swift wrote, 'Nobody made a greater mistake than he who did nothing because he could do only a little.' The issue of India's street children is so overwhelming that individuals, and even the leaders of quite large organisations, must often draw courage from this sentiment. It is so easy to despair, to think of one's own contribution as a mere 'drop in a bucket'. But Sathi can claim to be doing more than 'a drop'. To return some 7,000 children to their families in a year is a significant cup or even a small jug in the bucket of the total number of Indian children who run away from home each year.

More important, however, is that Sathi's work is based on a specific and not always accepted premise, namely that family and home is the best place for at least 90 per cent of all run away children who are persuaded by Sathi to return to their families. There are exceptions, and Sathi recognises this and has developed effective ways of ensuring that these children are entrusted to appropriate care givers; but for the great majority, home is best. Sathi is committed to this, not only on emotional grounds, but because their own results over 20 years, measured by the numbers of runaway children who have returned to their families and have remained with them, demonstrate that the premise is correct. If Sathi's case is accepted, then Sathi clearly has an opportunity and a duty, to expand its work dramatically, by itself or through other institutions.

Sathi has achieved remarkable results, in many different ways, and should for that reason continually question its own strategy; should Sathi carry on as it is doing, by doing more of the same, or should it focus on one of the many approaches which it has attempted, in order to achieve maximum impact? Because of Sathi's very success, it is not easy to choose any particular route, but it may be that some such focus would be the best way to use its limited resources, management and institutional capacity. This has to be done in the context of the whole Indian situation, not merely in order to expand the activities of Sathi itself; hence we must briefly examine the problem in India as a whole when we try crystal gazing for Sathi.

More of the Same—And Better

It is unlikely that the combined efforts of Sathi and all the other organisations which are working with runaways have any contact at all with more than 30 per cent of the children they are trying to assist. This is not satisfactory, particularly when Sathi has shown that it is possible to assist almost 7,000 children a year; the scale of the operation has long transcended what might have been achieved by a few gifted individuals. It has been systematised and organised on a large and replicable scale. Sathi could set itself a five-year target to expand to all of the 50—or, according to some authorities, 168—additional railway stations where large numbers of runaway boys tend to arrive, and to increase the outreach to cover a much larger percentage of runaway children arriving in railway stations. It might also be possible to extend outwards from railways stations to the potentially more dangerous and difficult streets outside, where there are almost certainly far more children than there are on the platforms.

Sathi has also shown that it is possible to 'infiltrate' the state child care system. Sathi could also try to extend this collaboration to all of the 400 or so major state children's homes in the country. This would help to ensure that far more runaway children return home within the stipulated four-month period. Thus, Sathi has enough of an agenda to grapple with even if it merely continues to do what it now does so well. Such a course of action is unlikely to satisfy an adventurous organisation like Sathi. Therefore, it is useful to look around to see what is changing and how these changes impact the lives of runaway children and the work of Sathi.

Reality at the Grassroots

One possibility is to switch focus from cure to prevention. For example, Railway Children, Sathi's major funding agency, commits to a preventive approach in its most recent strategy paper (2012–13) for India.

> We shall incorporate a preventive agenda into our restorative/rehabilitative approach, and focus on identifying strategic destination as well as source locations selected on the basis of baseline studies undertaken across India. We shall strive to facilitate a supportive family environment to prevent children from leaving home.

Sathi has been thinking ahead too. It has already taken several measures towards studying, and thus understanding and perhaps in time addressing the runaway problem at the source, that is, in the areas from which runaway children originate. A recent study by Sathi reveals the extent of the challenge.

In late 2011, Sathi undertook a survey of some 14 Gram Panchayats (between 65 to 70 villages) in Ranibennur Taluk, a vulnerable part of Haveri district in north Karnataka. A team of 53 researchers from Sathi itself, from a local NGO and from the community, identified a total of 450 children who could be described as children 'in need of care and protection' in terms of the JJ Act. Around 30 of these children were at work and not in school.

The findings (see Table 11.1) showed very dramatically that any institution which is concerned to assist children in need should not confine its attention to children on the streets or on railway platforms. They are perhaps the 'tip of the iceberg' and

Table 11.1:
Vulnerable Children in Ranibennur Taluk (Haveri District, Karnataka)

	No. of Children				
Gender	*In Families Seeking Government Institution or Hostel*	*Needing Food Supplements*	*Needing Medical Support*	*Needing Financial Support for Education*	*Total*
Boys	105	35	20	59	219
Girls	95	43	09	84	231
Total	200	78	29	143	450

Source: Findings of a survey by Sathi, December 2011.

far larger numbers, who are less obvious and less threatening to the rest of society, are still in their homes or whatever passes for their homes.

The study (see Table 11.1) revealed that the problems that commonly lead to children running away are widespread. There were large numbers of children 'in need of care and protection' who were still with the family and in some sense 'at home' and were thus unlikely to be noticed or cared for by official or non-government institutions.

The child welfare systems in countries like the UK, as we have seen, dig deeper, but not always with good effects, and actually take many children away from their homes. In India, however, resources are insufficient to allow the state to concern itself with what happens behind the walls of people's homes, whether the walls are made of stone or mud or plastic sheets, and it is unlikely that Indians' sense of personal privacy would allow the kind of intrusion that is normal in the UK. The Ranibennur Study, however, has shown Sathi that the problem is larger even than the large numbers of runaways would suggest.

The Macro Picture

A 2011 review of child protection systems for the period 2007 to 2012 by the Ministry of Women and Child Development

(MWCD), identified key concerns such as the major gaps in the qualitative and quantitative data on children in need of care and protection, the absence of standards for care, poor institutional infrastructure under the JJ system and the near complete absence of non-institutional and family-based care systems for children. A couple of years earlier in 2009–10, the Ministry had introduced the centrally-sponsored umbrella scheme, 'Integrated Child Protection Scheme' (ICPS) in order to address these very issues better and the implementation through the state governments was found to slow and uneven. One major achievement is that almost all states have initiated the programme and constituted statutory bodies for the purpose at state and district levels. There are 548 CWCs and 561 JJBs, 23 State Child Protection Societies (SCPS), 18 State Adoption Resource Agencies, 438 District Child Protection Societies (DCPS) in 16 states established under the Scheme. Childline 1098, a 24-hour telephone service is now available in 181 locations.

According to the strategic plan of the Ministry for the next five-year period, the ICPS is expected to support and encourage family based non-institutional care (adoption, sponsorship and foster care) as provided in the JJ Act. It is well accepted globally now that the child is best cared for in a family; but institutional care has remained, so far, the preferred option for many disadvantaged children in India. Often, children are exploited and abused in these institutions, and there are too many of them to be monitored effectively. There is, thus, a need to strengthen families so that the families are encouraged to keep their children within their safe environment; the ICPS recognises this formally and officially.

The priorities for the ICPS have been identified for the next five years (XII Plan Period 2012–17) and the foremost theme is the promotion of non-institutional care and promoting family and community-based care facilities. Existing homes for children will be upgraded to meet prescribed standards of care. Childline 1098 will be extended to all districts and cities. A credible database of children in difficult circumstances will be built for better planning of appropriate services. Similarly, the database for missing children will be developed and used for tracing them and restoring them to their families. Efforts will be made to strengthen families' capabilities to care for and protect their children. In all, this scheme is expected to usher in the professionalisation of child protection in India.

The independent National Commission for Protection of Child Rights (NCPCR) and State Commissions for the Protection of Child Rights (SCPCRs) will be allotted resources and staff to effectively fulfill their role and responsibility.

Other major schemes of the central government also formally recognise the needs of street children and have plans to address them. For example, the National Urban Health Mission (NUHM) plans to cater for the healthcare needs of street children. Mid-day meal centres are proposed at railway stations and bus stands to offer food to any child who walks in, along with a proper health check-up and distribution of appropriate medicines and identity cards. Similarly, bridge schools with quality education packages for street children who are out of the formal education system and vocational education and training for street children will also be provided. As with many other 'best laid plans' of the Government of India, the implementation has been delayed and patchy. We may expect that many of these plans will fructify where the state or local administration has the administrative and political will to make it happen for children.

For Sathi, the implications of this macro picture are encouraging. It is in the unique position of having the 'do-how' of shifting towards family and community based rehabilitation of runaway children. It has demonstrated the capacity slowly and surely to enter and to influence the institutions and statutory bodies that are emerging in this arena.

Options for Sathi

Should Sathi attempt to move further up the 'value chain', to try to deal with the problem at source, in villages and urban slums? This is perhaps the first of many strategic options that Sathi might consider. Sathi has already identified a number of areas from which many children run away, both in the south and in the states further north such as Bihar and the eastern part of Uttar Pradesh, which are sadly all too well known for their pervasive levels of poverty. Sathi has developed close links with thousands of households in these areas, and in some cases with the local CWCs, the police and other official institutions, through its successful efforts to link runaway children with their families. It might be possible to build on these links, to attempt to work with more families in the major origin areas, and thus to prevent runaways by addressing the problem at the source as well as by 'closing the stable door after the horse has bolted'.

As is so often the case, money is not a problem. The central government schemes described earlier are well funded and there are many well-designed programmes to tackle the issue. The difficulty is with the 'last mile' at the state, district or village levels through which assistance has to be delivered. The potential recipients are unaware of their entitlements. The field staff of local authorities through whom the programmes should be available have other pre-occupations and priorities. 'Facilitation' is all that is needed. This may mean a wide variety of actions, ranging from simple information to introductions and even to writing out the forms for clients or organising them to be able to claim their entitlements. The main role of many NGOs is not actually to provide assistance, but to facilitate people's access to it. The poorest and the most marginalised people whose children are most likely to have run away are generally those who most need assistance, and whose access to it needs the most 'facilitation'.

Sathi might therefore choose to extend its field presence out from railway platforms into the slums and villages from which its children have come. Sathi attempts to support the families to which children have returned after running away, and to help them to address the problems which had caused their children to leave. Sathi could then also reach out to families whose children may be the next to run away. The families whom Sathi has already helped could be the best advisers to other families whose children may be at risk of running away, and their children who have had the experience of running away and have returned could also advise other children not to follow their example.

This would surely need a massive increase in the scope and size of Sathi's operations.

Another option which emerges for Sathi is the opportunity arising from government plans to set up administrative and statutory bodies especially for child protection in each district in the country. Sathi can develop criteria to select locations and work to establish genuinely child-friendly practices in these relatively new functions of the government. The Ministry acknowledges the need for close collaboration and partnerships with civil society to meet the needs of children. Sathi's pioneering efforts with the CWCs and the government children's homes provides a functional template for working with the district level child protection units. Similarly, it has already begun to work with Special Juvenile Police Units (SJPUs) in railway stations and this too can be extended to the juvenile police units proposed in each district. It can continue to concentrate on assisting the state to do what is after all a rather fundamental role of any civilized state—the care of children whose families are temporarily or on a longer term unable or unwilling to take care of them. Sathi believes in the quality of its own work, but keeps a low profile and tries its best to serve children in need by sharing and transferring its own learning and skills to government staff. By doing so, it would in time put 'itself out of business' or move to the next deeper challenge.

What to Expect in Railway Stations

There are working and scalable models which demonstrate how the railway station can become child-friendly and safe for children. The policy and strategy papers indicate that there will be improvements in the 50 major stations across India. Many of them will have a drop-in shelter for platform children, a Special Juvenile Police Unit of the Railway Police Force or the Government Railway Police, food security offered by the Integrated Child Development Services, care and protection organised by the CWCs which meet at least a few times in the railway station, a good data base on children found on railway platforms, and access to NGO services.

Sathi's model of platform work aimed at family reunification is equally well established and exists side by side with the other success stories of effective support to children on platforms. There are visible signs of change on railway platforms. The old image that the police hold of boys on the platform, as dishonest or criminally inclined is slowly changing. The tightening of security in large stations has helped them distinguish between harmless boys and those with connections to criminal elements. Perhaps, in response to efforts by Sathi and others, railway police are already identifying newly arrived runaway children and trying to help them, arranging for them to be properly taken care of. The NGO campaigns to persuade the railway police to set up special units to take care of children on main railway stations seem likely to succeed, and this should radically alter the whole national approach to the care of children who arrive on railway platforms. There are no official short-term shelters near the railway stations such as those run by NGOs. It does seem feasible that government children's homes might in future open outreach centers of this sort. The railway police can also extend their dedicated children's reception centres on platforms so that they could also act as short-term night shelters.

The whole Sathi system could thus be taken over by official institutions, and in theory, they could do the job as well as Sathi itself or any other NGO. The railway police, the CWCs with their links to committees throughout India and the government children's homes have the wherewithal and the networks to deal with every stage in the chain. However, it is not in the nature of government institutions to work with the same flexibility and humanity that is needed; this may be the major challenge.

In the proposals and plans for changes in railway stations there is hardly any direct reference to the possibility of family reunification as a long-term effective solution, in keeping with the provisions of the law and the strategic direction set. Sathi has the opportunity to offer its expertise in identifying the different categories of children on the platform, child guidance, address tracing, family counselling and actual family reunification.

So far Sathi's effort has been to take these to other NGOs already working on the platforms. With the anticipated increase in the pressure on the police and the railway administrators to offer greater protection to platform children, Sathi can expect greater acceptance and can begin working more intensively with them.

The Future of Government Homes

In the next five years, the facilities and care provided to children in government homes is expected to improve with clarity about standards and closer monitoring. Homes run by NGOs and others will also be supervised and regulated. The isolation and power-lessness of children within these institutions is perhaps the biggest factor which allows abuses to go unchecked. The access provided by the CWCs has opened up these institutions to scrutiny by civil society which can now work within the Homes to promote better quality of care and protection. Sathi has a unique contribution to make in this scenario. It is one of the few national NGOs with no interest in creating its own infrastructure for child care and therefore stays free of any conflict of interests when dealing with CWCs, government homes and other 'fit' institutions.

Sathi can offer two unique services—tracing addresses to reunite children with their families and Sathi camps to help the children recover their lost childhood and set their course for the future. Sathi is one of the few organizations which see government homes as transit points rather than destinations in these children's lives. Children's personal habits are hard to correct and the Sathi camp is an effective in helping a child overcome these habits. The caretakers in large government homes say that they are forced to take harsh measures for discipline in these homes because children in the grip of substance abuse cannot be trusted. The Sathi camp offers a way to take children beyond these bad habits and helps them settle down emotionally. These two services do not need any change at the macro level and Sathi only needs to enlarge its own scale by accessing financial and human resources and creating a pool of people within the sector who can run these camps and innovate further. In offering these services to the government homes Sathi can quickly increase the number of children it reunites with families and can also improve its outreach to girls.

Partnerships and Advocacy

As we saw earlier, Sathi has tried to expand its work by partnering with other NGOs. At the time of writing, Sathi was still in partnership with three institutions, but the majority of these arrangements had been discontinued. This is no doubt that the 30 odd NGOs with which Sathi has worked have learned something from the experience. It cannot, however, be claimed that these partnerships have been a very effective way for Sathi to extend its outreach. It would be ideal if Sathi could remain at its present scale, or even become somewhat smaller, and play the role of a research, learning and innovation centre and a source of new ideas, while large numbers of imitators or 'franchisees' applied its methods, and improved on them throughout India and even further afield. In recent years, some of the senior staff members have moved out and set up their own operations to work with children. Such Sathi 'clones' can continue to use the basic Sathi approach with specific adaptations to suit local and regional variations.

Sathi's approach of bearing the costs and sending its own expert staff to demonstrate family reunification seems in practice to make its partner NGOs feel that Sathi wants to 'take them over' and impose its own ideas on them. This makes Sathi's services 'supply-driven' rather than 'demand-led' and is therefore unsustainable in the longer run. Effective and long-lasting partnerships will only develop if the partner institutions see Sathi's family reunification strategy and other techniques as useful 'plug-ins' which can supplement their own work rather than displacing it.

Innovation Hub

Sathi should retain and build on its 'comparative advantage' in its own innovations—platform work, shelters, family reunification and Sathi camps. These are uniquely effective models, which merit far wider replication and Sathi may be able to offer its expertise as an advisory service which is sought and paid for by the actual user—be it an NGO or a government home or even agencies in other countries. In addition it can continue to generate new services which specifically address the needs of these children. Fostering, for example, is widely used in the UK and elsewhere. It is not perfect, but it is *prima facie* preferable for a young person to be in a family than in an institution, and fostering can be organised so that it is safe and supportive. Additionally, it is much less expensive than traditional institutions; it is very rare when a preferable solution to a social problem is also more economical than the alternative, but fostering is a case in point.

It should be possible for Sathi to obtain funding for a significant experiment with fostering, which could test once and for all, the rather general assumption that 'fostering won't work in India'. This assumption is based in part on the fact that Indian children often live with members of their extended family rather than with their natural parents, and that this informal fostering is far more effective than any formal system such as those used elsewhere. There is some truth in this, as it is also true that many old people in India live with their children and grandchildren, so that there is not the same need for old people's homes as there is in more fractured societies.

Since 1992 Sathi has convincingly demonstrated that most runaway children can go home, and will stay there and benefit if they do. There is and probably never will be total agreement on where to draw the line, on how bad a home must be for a child to benefit more from being kept in an institution, but there are alternatives like fostering and sponsorship, which are not widely used in India as of now. Sathi can take the lead to develop these options. Fostering outside the extended family could be a solution to stabilise a child who has been through various experiences on the platform. Sathi is ideally positioned to experiment with this.

Such an experiment could be based on a study of experiences in India and elsewhere, as well as on Sathi's own knowledge of how families have successfully reintegrated runaways. It could involve the many families whose children have benefitted from Sathi's intervention. It might be possible for Sathi to contact these parents, who are often very grateful to Sathi and who wish to pay something back to them and to society for the assistance they and their child have received. Such families might be willing to take on one more homeless and difficult child, and Sathi could develop a menu of good practices, and then implement a family fostering programme to demonstrate what could be done. This could include some payments to the foster families, to cover their out-of-pocket expenses and possibly also some recompense for their trouble. Such payments, and the associated administrative costs, would almost certainly be well below the very high cost of accommodating children in government homes.

There is also a pressing need for more data about the various categories of children in need of care and protection. These systems should go beyond simple communication of individual cases to record and coordinate information so that it can be accessed by all the relevant institutions. Sathi's managerial approach to data capture and analysis qualifies it ideally to take a lead in this. Sathi's staff members themselves are acutely aware of the need for a portal which could act as a child tracking system. It could link police reports of missing children to records of arrivals at government homes, and it could be used by the railway police and other institutions such as Sathi itself which often have the first 'official' contact with runaway children. This could save a great amount of time and anguish for the parents. If Sathi platform staff could log into a portal which told them that a child whom they had contacted might be one who had been reported to have run away, this could in some cases obviate the need for the lengthy process of finding out from a child where he has come from, or at least materially shorten it. Such a system could also be extended to include children who have been through Sathi's own processes, or have moved on from government or NGO or Children's Homes. Right now, most of these homes have no record of what happens to children who have left them.

Sathi as a Catalyst

One vital difference between commercial businesses and genuine social enterprises is that the former focus on their own growth while the latter focus on the achievement of their mission, irrespective of which institution achieves it. Sathi is by no means perfect, but its work in its first 20 years has shown that it does not share this weakness for promoting its own growth, rather than the achievement of its objective. Sathi's leaders are self-effacing personally, and Sathi as an institution works quite overtly to put itself out of business.

It can be argued that government itself will never be able to take over the functions which Sathi and other NGOs perform, and also that government's resources, or the resources they are willing to devote to this problem, will never be sufficient to cover the full cost. As in the UK and in other richer countries, there will always be a need for voluntary action and voluntary donations. Even if one takes the more optimistic view, that the Government of India will in due course be willing and able to take over the full cost of funding child care, this will obviously take many years to achieve. In the meantime, non-government institutions, with voluntary funding, will have to bear a large part of the load.

The best way to persuade society in general, and the government, to be more aware of the problem of runaway children, and to adopt more effective ways of dealing with it, is to demonstrate by example. Sathi is already providing examples of good practice in plenty. The lessons Sathi has learned must also be widely disseminated so that others can be aware of them, can see them and can adopt them easily. In spite of its inherent institutional modesty, Sathi can continue and expand its 'advocacy'. This book can play a small part of this task. Even if only one runaway child goes home, rather than remaining on a railway platform or in an institution, because someone read the book, it will have been a worthwhile endeavour.

References

Internet

Railway children. 2010. 'Envisioning our future—Making India a Child Friendly Nation', shared with author during an interview with Railway Children India http://www.railwaychildren.org.uk/article.asp?id=658&highlight=strategy paper.

Reports

MWCD. 2012. 'Report of the Working Group on Child Rights for the Twelfth Five Year Plan 2012–2017.' New Delhi.
UNICEF. 2010. Country Office Annual Report. India.

Annexure: The Sathi Story and Civil Society's Response to Children's Needs

Children's Participation—Precept and Practice

Early Years in Raichur

As long as anyone could remember there had always been a few ragged children hanging around the railway station in Raichur, a small district town in northern Karnataka. They begged, scavenged for scraps of food or helped the porters and the vendors, and maybe they stole too. This was no different from almost any railway station in India and most passengers tried to ignore them, or to brush them away. It is never comfortable to be reminded of how unfortunate some of your fellow-citizens are.

In 1992, Kamala, a young social work graduate from Raichur, returned to her home town after completing her studies. She was not sure exactly what to do, but she was clear that she wanted in some way to work for the benefit of children. She asked Pramod Kulkarni for his advice. He was the Founder and Head of Prerana, a rural development NGO based in Raichur. He had graduated from the Indian Institute of Management, Ahmedabad, India's leading business school, and had then worked in Bihar and Jharkhand for Pradan, a major rural livelihoods support institution. In 1990, he moved back to Karnataka, his home state, and started a new organisation, 'Prerana', in Raichur. Prerana worked with poor farmers on community based irrigation projects.

Prerana was not working with children, but when Kamala approached him, Pramod Kulkarni reminded her that there were a number of obviously needy children to be seen every day at the railway station. Could she not try to do something for them?

Kamala liked the idea, and made a few enquiries, but she moved away from Raichur before actually starting anything. Pramod's interest had however been kindled and he suggested that Vinod Fetardo, an enthusiastic new staff member at Prerana, should pick up the activity. Vinod soon became committed to this work. He spent time on the Raichur station platform and got to know some of the children who lived there. It became his routine to visit the platform and talk to the children. He saw many children in unhealthy and unhygienic settings. Some boys had injuries and cuts on their bodies. He soon realised they needed medical assistance and began carrying a first-aid kit with him. Eventually, he persuaded three or four boys to leave the platform and live in the Prerana office. This could not continue for very long, and Vinod quickly realised that he had to find a proper place for the children to shelter.

It was hard to find a place in Raichur. Nobody wanted to lease out their building for such 'rough and rowdy' boys. At first they tried an isolated house on a small hill, but this was too far from the station. Then they found a place closer to the station. It was in an unsavoury part of the town but it served the purpose. The boys could come and go as they pleased; they continued to earn whatever they could on the station or elsewhere; the older boys managed the shelter, kept it clean and contributed some money towards food. Vinod and a colleague from Prerana who had also become involved with the idea lived in the shelter and got to know the boys quite well.

The purpose was to offer unconditional acceptance and to bring the boys back to mainstream society. If the children stayed there for a reasonable time, the staff thought, they would come to depend on the emotional support in a positive way. But the children kept moving, because their life on the platform was almost nomadic; it was life on the railways, not on any particular station. As the children moved, the staff followed them, and they set up similar shelters at the stations in nearby towns. Within a year, they were working in three other stations, based on what the children in Raichur had told them. This work was put under a separate budget in Prerana, and by 1993 the railway children activity was costing around ₹60,000 (US$ 1,500) a year.

They received several in-kind donations of food, clothing and so on; Community Aid Abroad, Pune and Save the Children, Canada, also provided some support. The Sathi staff began to discover the social networks of children on platforms. Some of them did not actually live on the platform at all. They came there every day from neighbouring slums. A small 'hard core' actually lived full time on the platform, and had been living there for some time, but the majority had not been there for more than a few days. They had arrived, had a taste of platform life, and either moved on by jumping on to another train or walked out into the town, or had perhaps made their own way back home if they knew how to get there. They found that the boys formed gangs around the kind of work they did and they supported and protected their members. They spent their days playing, fighting, sharing food and drugs, earning some money when they could and going to the movies; their independent counter-culture shocked most 'normal' people who observed them as they passed through the railway stations. Prerana staff learned how to identify and understand these relationships, the problems and the pleasures. They also protected the younger children from harassment by the police. At this point the staff had no real focus to their work. All they wanted to do was to make life somewhat more tolerable for the children they met on the platforms, by providing them with a secure shelter, food and some affection.

Mama Devi was the first woman to join the team in 1993. She had trained in community work in a government programme and was studying law. She worked with Sathi till recently, and has now left after stabilizing Sathi's counselling serives for girls in GCH in Delhi. Basvaraj Shali, who is now Deputy Secretary in charge of all Sathi's operations, also joined in May 1993. He had studied sociology, and had been working as a part-time lecturer, but his major interest was in working with young people. As a student, he had been active in the National Cadet Corps (NCC) and the National Service Scheme (NSS), and he was continuing his youth work in his home village, close to the town of Wadi near Raichur. He opened a shelter near Wadi railway station as soon as he joined and had soon attracted about 25 children who were regulars on the platform at Wadi. The station acted as a 'hub'. Children who lived there set out each morning to other neighbouring stations where they earned money in various ways. They came back in the evening and got together to enjoy their day's earnings. Basavaraj has expanded the work to the national level building networks and managing the operations as they expanded.

Vinod, Basavaraj and Mama worked closely together. Pramod Kulkarni was not directly involved, since he was fully occupied with Prerana's rural development work, but he was their support and guide. He helped them to raise the money they needed and he closely monitored their progress. They tried various activities to engage the children and to keep them interested in staying at the shelter. One favourite was to organise picnics in the countryside, but one early attempt nearly ended in disaster.

The team had rented a small bus, but as the children were climbing into it, a policeman, who knew some of the boys all too well, asked where they were going, and why. One child, who was not very keen on joining, said that they were being abducted. The police at once told the children to get off the bus, and arrested the three team members. The children ran back to the relative safety of the station, and after lengthy explanations the police released the team. This incident actually helped the team in the end, because it made their work more widely known and the railway police understood what they were about. On another occasion, the boys who used the Wadi shelter made a huge Ganesh idol and performed the 10-day festival and procession. This strengthened the children's confidence and their sense of belonging, and it also brought the work of the Prerana team to the attention of the local community.

At this stage the main aim of the project was to help the boys find more secure jobs away from the station platforms. Many boys were placed in local businesses such as tea shops, carpentry workshops, mechanics and garages. Shali recalls organising donation of shoe polishing kits to some boys who wanted to do this work on trains. When the Sathi team looks back at those early days, they marvel that it never occurred to them that they were in fact supporting child labour.

The boys did well and their employers treated them well, but the team found that the boys soon became restless. Some of them went back to the platforms, and some even went back to their homes. These incidents showed the team what they should be doing. The team began to understand that the children had a deep need for their families. Shri Deep Purkayastha, Director, Prajak, Kolkata shared a similar experience in his organisation. Prajak's initial effort was to work on the emotional needs of children in Government Homes using experiential methodologies like psycho-drama. Children used these opportunities to express their need to reconnect with their families. The organisation remains committed to family reunification and believe that it works in 70 per cent of the cases.

Discovering the Child's Need for Home

The staff continued and extended the picnics to last two or three days and they experimented with different games and other life-skills activities in the picnics. Even a short experience of this kind was enough to make a child decide to move away from the platform and settle down to some work. The weekend picnics were lengthened to a carefully structured full week's programme of life-skills training, and many of the boys were deeply influenced by it. Sathi's founders realised that many children who had been away from home for some time had become accustomed to their life on the railway platform or the street. Many had become habituated to drugs, or substances like cigarettes, betel or sniffing glue or solvents, or to sexual excitement. Their dangerous liberated life in itself had become a habit; human beings are good at adapting to new circumstances and it can be difficult to return to the environment which they may initially have been very reluctant to leave behind. Such children would not go home at once, but they needed to be removed from their platform life to a novel, neutral, secure, interesting and yet challenging environment, where they could be counselled and could become more self-aware, and could realise again that what they really wanted was to be at home.

In 1994, the team, who had by this time started to call themselves Sathi, meaning 'Friend' or 'Companion', came into contact with Father George Kollashany of the Don Bosco order who was a pioneer in working with street children. They worked with him and Dr Shekar Seshadri of the National Institute for Mental Health and Neurosciences (NIMHANS) in Bangalore to design and run a full-scale camp for runaway children which would help the children to rediscover their childhood. It was hard work. The focus was to help the children to shake off the bad habits they had formed on the platforms and to assist them to come back into the mainstream of society. At the end of the camp, each boy chose what kind of work he wanted to do, and the team helped them to get into that line of work. Many proved to be excellent employees. There were a few who started their own businesses, and Sathi often provided the equipment and money they needed.

Most of the boys renewed their links with their families once they had steadied themselves financially, and the Sathi team realised that many of the children who had said they were orphans actually did have families. Some boys had a very clear memory of their families and homes, including their addresses and phone numbers. Once they had become more self-confident and had saved some money, they began to express an interest in going home. The team found again and again that most children had a deep longing to go home, not to start a new life elsewhere. Most of them had in any case run away for quite minor reasons. If Sathi could help them and their families to overcome the barriers which they had built by the very act of running away, the children could be happily reunited with their families.

In 2000, the Sathi team heard from a few platform boys that some boys from Karnataka were being held in a government children's home in Pune against their will. Again the theme was that they wanted to go home but were not allowed to leave. Sathi contacted the management of the home and demonstrated how they could trace children's families and get them safely home. This laid the foundation for Sathi's continued engagement with government homes and similar institutions. The conviction also grew that runaway boys on platforms on deeper reflection truly wanted to return to their families even though they seemed to enjoy their chaotic lives. Thus, Sathi's theme of reuniting boys with their families came from their direct experiences with railway children, working children as well as children in institutions. It was not based on some abstract ideal notions but relied on the behaviour of children and their parents as well as the realisation that institutions were often worse than the family or school.

Since then, Sathi has demonstrated many times over that even children who have been institutionalised for many years in government residential homes and have been long separated from their families can successfully be reunited. Under the Juvenile Justice Act of 2006, these government homes are expected as a first priority to find the families of the children in their care within three months and to send them home. This has not happened in a systematic way in most homes and Sathi has developed an effective and sensitive process which often succeeds where the staff of the government homes is able to make little headway.

Formation of Sathi

By 1998, it had become clear that Prerana's children's project, Sathi, had to have its own institutional identity. Sathi was registered as an independent society, and the funds that had been raised for its activities were transferred to the new entity. This happened to coincide with a lull in Prerana's main activity, so Pramod Kulkarni was able to work full time for Sathi for the five years between 1998 and 2003.

The Sathi team was by this time fully convinced that most children would with some guidance want to go back to their families, and that their families would welcome and cherish their child who came back to them. They continued to organise camps for all the children they met at the various stations, but it was becoming clear that if a boy could be guided away from platform life before he became accustomed to it, he could easily resume his family life, without any need for a camp. They needed to meet children quickly, before they were 'sucked into' the platform community.

This faith in the capacity of the family to nurture and regenerate was put to a tough test when Sathi ventured to reunite minor girls rescued from the sex trade in Mumbai with their families in Karnataka in the year 2001–02. These girls had been trafficked and sold and found in Mumbai. The rescued girls were accommodated in Kasturba Girls Home in Mumbai. The home officials entrusted Sathi with this delicate task of tracing the addresses and reuniting the girls from Karnataka with their families. Out of the 100 or so girls who were from Karnataka, Sathi was able to trace home addresses and locate the families for nearly 71. The families were informed about their daughters having been found and in most cases the exact circumstances were shared at least with the mothers. The families were very happy to take them back and many girls were able to resume ordinary lives. The follow-up showed that 65 of the rescued girls stayed with their own or immediate families. Eleven of them were married and 63 have taken up some kind of meaningful work. Six of them could not be traced and are believed to have run away from home.

This was again an experience where Sathi's willingness to trust the strength of family bonds was amply justified. Middle class urban notions of morality were obviously not operating in this backward region, where ritual prostitution traditions have been common in the past.

Early Intervention and Reunion

Pramod Kulkarni has a passion for methodical documentation, which is by no means usual in NGOs, particularly those dealing in such an emotive area as children's welfare. Kulkarni himself and all his colleagues at Sathi were personally convinced that reunion with family was the best solution for most run away children, but this was not enough. By 2000, Sathi was helping around 700 children a year. They contacted a large sample of the children who had been sent home since 1998, and found that over 80 per cent had stayed at home. This confirmed their belief in what they had been doing.

In 2000, based on research and analysis, Sathi determined to focus their work on what was called the 'early intervention' strategy. This was first tried in Pune. Rather than trying to get to know the hard core of long-term resident children on the platforms, Sathi staff walked up and down the platform when major trains arrived, looking out for children who seemed to be on their own. They would then invite the child to the Sathi shelter and gently try to find out where they had come from. Many of the children were quickly and happily reunited with their families, sometimes even in a few hours, as their families had been desperately hunting for their lost child.

It was clear that the most productive way to help most children was to help them get home. Many did not know where home was, or how to get there, and some were frightened to go home. A few had merely been separated from their families when visiting a crowded market, *mela* or a religious festival, but most had run away on purpose for some reason or other. Whatever the cause, it might still discourage them from returning, and the very act of running away was also a serious misdeed for which a child could expect to be punished. Fear of punishment for having run away has always been a major disincentive for children to go home, and much of Sathi's repatriation process is designed to overcome it.

The team continued to help children who were on the platform. They also started to develop and share specific techniques whereby children could be helped to find out where their homes were, to communicate with their families, and, if possible, to arrange to go home. In the early days, staff had to rely on the post, or sometimes on telegrams, and many if not most families in urban slums or rural villages have no formal postal addresses. The recent wide availability of mobile telephones has made this much easier, and quicker. This technological change has in itself helped Sathi to shift its emphasis from helping children on the platforms to helping them to go home.

The Sathi team was excited by their success in getting children home, and they wanted to spread it to as many locations as possible, so they decided to try to persuade other NGOs which were working with platform children to adopt the same approach. ActionAid was convinced that this was a significant step forward and they set up a group of NGOs in Andhra Pradesh to extend the practice. Sathi helped these NGOs to start similar work on seven railway stations in the State, and Sathi started a partnership in Mumbai with Saathi, its namesake with a double 'a'. The early intervention method was also adopted by other NGOs in Itarsi, Kolkata and Jhansi.

Spreading the Method

By 2001, the Sathi team was convinced that it was on the right track. Their work confirmed that children arriving on railway platforms were emotionally vulnerable; early intervention saved them from pain and hardship. The close-knit communities of children on the platforms, with their strong sense of belonging often demanded a high emotional physical and even financial price for membership. They lived precariously, exposed to a host of risks and hardships. In the best interest of the child and the family, the priority for well wishers like Sathi, is to move them off platforms to safer places as soon as they arrive off a train. Until they can be and are willing to be moved to a better place, the priority is to provide them with food, a place to wash and to sleep, and above all to be secure.

Sathi's staff take the view that running away is often a part of the natural rebellion that accompanies the transition from child-hood to adulthood; they do not try to decide who is to blame for the child running away, but only to understand and then to improve the situation and bridge the gaps in communication and understanding. Most children realize that they have made a mistake when they arrive on a station platform; they are glad to go back home if there is an understanding person who will help them to do so. Their families are also shocked when a child runs away; they come to recognize his needs, perhaps for the first time. They realize how important their child is to them and make an effort to relate more closely and nurture the child. Sathi's main task is in essence quite simple; to relate personally to every child they meet, and help him to decide to go home, or, less often, to get away from the platform. Even the 'veterans' on the street or platform want to go back to their families and their homes, and they too value the chance of a new start offered to them through the Sathi camps.

From 1998 until 2004, Sathi continued to focus its efforts on spreading the early intervention and family reunion strategy. The team was surprised to find that not everyone had the same level of faith in the ability of families to care for their children. Pramod Kulkarni and his colleagues remembered their own childhood and the love and care that they had received, and they found it hard to understand why other people should not share their view that home was the best place for all children. They rigorously examined their own faith in this approach, and studied why some children decided to leave home, what happened when they returned, the actual situation in the family and the success or otherwise of the reunion. They started systematically to follow up as many children as they could by phone or other contacts, and they found that around nine out of every 10 children stayed at home.

By this time the Sathi shelters had ceased to be 'drop-in' centres for long-term platform children; they had become short-term places for lost or runaway children to stay while Sathi's staff tried to find out where they came from and persuade the children and their families to come together again. Sathi was clear that they did not want to have any physical infrastructure such as institutions for the longer term care of children. They developed good ties with other NGOs which have such institutions, and with the government home, and they could when necessary send children to such facilities.

Unlike other organizations which run schools or vocational training institutions, Sathi did not believe in 'formal' classrooms, for children, for their own staff or for the staff of partner NGOs. They relied on learning by doing; an experienced staff member from Sathi was seconded to new partner organizations to demonstrate the Sathi method. Partner NGOs also liked the Sathi camp methodology, but it was not readily adopted. Many NGOs are proud of their own ideas, and they are reluctant to learn from others, particularly when their own staff's training and their physical facilities such as schools and long term children's homes are designed for a quite different approach. Change is not always welcome. Thus Sathi is today somewhat disenchanted with its partnership model and prefers to invest time and energy in working with the government system.

Growth and the Move to Bangalore

In 2004 Sathi shifted its headquarters from Raichur to Bangalore, signalling their ambition to act on a larger scale. By this time Sathi had employed 40 members as staff. They worked under the overall guidance of Pramod Kulkarni. In the early days, each team member could step in to perform any task that needed to be done. As the programme became more complex, people were hired for specific jobs rather than as generalists. By 2011, there were almost 100 staff, working in 20 different towns. In each shelter there is one person in charge, with a small team of platform outreach staff, specialist counsellors and the shelter teachers who do non-formal education. There is also one office assistant and a person in charge of documentation. Similarly in the camps there is a camp coordinator, at least three camp staff, and counsellors, teachers, a cook and housekeeper. There are also some counsellors who are attached to government homes.

This move gave Sathi a greater exposure to others engaged in similar work. This prompted them to try and apply their methods to street children in urban slums. Most of the children were with families or in close touch, but were left uncared for. Thus children who were persuaded to give up bad habits and behaviour soon reverted to earlier habits because of the influence of their neighbourhood. After a few years of this work Sathi chose to stay focused on the children separated from families on railway platforms. The move and each attempt to collaborate helped them refine their methods further. They sharpened their focus on advocacy and research in order to complement their 'field' work on the station platforms.

Action Learning and Research

Through these years Sathi has continued to ask critical questions of itself and its work and at any given moment there are a few action learning projects in progress within the organization. Over the last 10 years it has made consistent effort to interest external scholars to study issues of relevance by offering fellowships to study a variety of themes. One common element in these research projects is that the topic and the field explorations are closely linked to the operations of Sathi and have the possibility of offering them clarity, ideas and insights.

One question it has continually engaged with is to ask why children run away. Is it poverty? Is it deep dissatisfaction or some form of abuse at home? Sathi continues this research and is not ready to accept speculations about this key question. The answers it found have become the basis for deciding whether or not they should be helped to return home, and, if they should, how best to help them. There are obviously many different reasons, and it is not easy to get the right answer easily. To begin with children themselves often make up fanciful and sometimes terrible stories to justify what they have done and to impress an audience.

Jayesh had begun with a horrifying story. His father and elder brother had been murdered by a man and the same person had kidnapped him, brought him to Delhi and abandoned him in the bus stand near the railway station. He had been hungry and thirsty and had come to the station looking for food. He soon admitted the truth, however. He had run away from his uncle's place where he had been staying in order to attend school, because he hated studying and wanted to return to his mother and brothers.

On many occasions, Sathi staff members have persevered and found that when they get to know a child, his story changes and becomes closer to the truth. It is perhaps not surprising that there is so little data on this subject. Sathi documents the shifts in the stories of children they work closely with. The quality of data especially from the camps is reliable because the staff have the time to relate with the children, gain their confidence and get as close to the truth as possible. These sources are made available to interested researchers. The staff also take up their own research projects.

This research has found that many if not most children leave home for quite trivial reasons. A scolding or even fear of scolding or physical punishment from their parents is enough to trigger running away.

Eight-year-old Pradeep had run away because he had had a fight with his classmate and unintentionally injured him. He was afraid that the boy's father would beat him up. Divakar had been scolded by his mother for asking their neighbours for money, so he left home. Pratap had left home because the cattle he had been minding had strayed into his neighbours' field; he had thought that the animals had gone missing and that he would be punished.

In 2008, when he was 11 years old, Nilesh, who lives in a middle class area of Bangalore, had tried to cut his own hair so that he would look like a film star. He had made a total mess of it, and when she saw him his mother lost her temper, slapped him soundly and said 'Get out of my sight!' He took her literally, and ran out of the house down to Bangalore railway station. He had previously been on a holiday to his family's native place in Chitoor, a six-hours' train journey, and he planned to go there again. A Sathi outreach worker saw him wandering about the railway station and persuaded him to come with her to the Sathi shelter. He stayed there for three days, telling a variety of tall tales about where he had come from and why. He enjoyed playing with the other children in the shelter, but then he realised that it would be better to go home, so he gave the staff his family's phone number and they took him home. They were overjoyed to have him back, and he continues to be a good student in an expensive English medium school. He is quite sure that he won't run away again, and wants to help other children by talking to them in Sathi's shelter or in government institutions, to show them it's better to go home.

Many boys leave home in search for work. Some run away from problems at work.

Jayanth had left home without anyone's knowledge to search for work and freedom because he did not like being scolded for having made trivial mistakes when he was doing household chores. Shakeel had run away from home because he had been beaten by his employer. Anuj had left because his employer used to send him out on boring errands instead of allowing him to learn to be a tailor which was what he enjoyed.

Other children leave home because they want to see the bright lights of the city, to find adventure and excitement and some boys leave home merely because they are bored. Other children are unhappy at school, or in the hostels where their parents have sent them to enable them to attend better schools than are available near their homes. Pressure to complete homework, fear of showing a poor report card, and abuse and bullying in hostels are some of the common reasons which children give for having run away. Many children from poor families are sent to hostels run by religious orders, and they run away because they dislike the strict discipline or are bullied by senior students.

HR Challenges

The staff work long hours, often under considerable stress. They are inspired by the affection they receive from the children and by the transformation they help to bring to the children's lives. They have come to see that children who run away face many challenges. A disturbed family situation, a father's alcoholism, fear of punishment, or even pressure from friends may have prompted them to leave home. The staff members believe that their most important contribution is to protect these very vulnerable children, and to guide them to return to their families and resume their education.

It is hard for Sathi to find and to retain the right people for this work. All the staff have to be generous enough to accept and respect children who are viewed with suspicion and hostility by most of us. Nearly every staff member can recall occasions when children in their charge have been very difficult to handle. Resilience and capacity for affection cannot be captured on résumés or developed through education. They have to be familiar with local languages and place names and in the region where they are to work. It is most unlikely that families will ever pay for having their children restored to them, so there are no income generation opportunities or 'sustainability' for Sathi. It has to depend entirely on grants and the salaries are modest even by NGO standards. This is difficult, because the work on the platform, in the camps or in government homes can be physically and emotionally very demanding. It is a bigger challenge when Sathi needs managers, trained social workers, counsellors, documentation specialists and so on.

New recruits also have difficulties with Sathi's organization culture. It is not a place for fiery activists. Sathi prefers to maintain a low profile and avoids direct confrontation with the establishment, such as the railway police or the management of government children's homes. It prefers to work with these agencies, to change them from within. Sathi is also very willing to admit its own mistakes, to learn from them and to change its methods, having shifted radically away from its original use of part time shelters and picnics for long-term platform children. This soft approach can be very frustrating for idealists who prefer to campaign openly for changing the many dysfunctional aspects of existing systems and institutions. Sathi's work is based on their quite simple belief in the family as the 'best' place for a child. This may not seem radical enough to some young professionals. Sathi's whole approach is in some ways counter-intuitive and very different from the dominant discourse of child rights activism.

Sathi's Networks and Coverage

Sathi's unusual approach is very different from that of many of the high profile Indian NGOs. It is not identified with any one 'charismatic leader', it does not campaign visibly or loudly, and it works closely with government, rather than against it. Nevertheless, Sathi has developed long standing relationships with both Indian and foreign funding agencies. Specialized donors for children's causes, whose staff understand the subtleties of working with children in India, have consistently supported Sathi's work.

Railway Children is a UK-based charity which works for homeless children in India, east Africa, and in the UK. They agree with Sathi that early intervention is crucial to protect children from harm, and they see Sathi's camps, and their family reunions, as well as its close collaboration with government and police, as examples for similar work elsewhere in the world. They have funded Sathi and some other local organizations in India since 1996, and Sathi expects this partnership to continue. Every Child is another international agency which works in 14 countries and has been supporting Sathi's camps and family reunions over the last seven years. They see these as innovations worth replicating. They are likely to continue their support. They also appreciate Sathi's openness to partnerships and collaborations.

Sathi obtains around half of its funding from Indian sources. The Sir Ratan Tata Trust (SRTT), supported all aspects of Sathi's work for 15 years, and they particularly appreciated Sathi's commitment to learn continuously from experience, and to change and improve its services. The Sir Dorabji Tata Trust (SDTT), a larger trust of the House of Tatas has recently begun to support Sathi's work with government children's homes and the CWCs, and the Azim Premji family also supports Sathi's camps and family reunions. Child Rights and You (CRY) had also supported Sathi in the initial years.

Sathi has no funding from the government or the railways. Sathi's work of family reunions does not fit into any existing 'scheme' of the government for the welfare of street children like the Integrated Programme for Street Children (IPSC). Sathi's finds the bureaucratic and other problems of dealing with government funding too onerous in relation to the amounts that are likely to be obtained. It seems paradoxical, however, and uneconomic, that there is money to cover the cost of taking care of children who are away from home but nothing to fund their return to their homes. Non-government and foreign donors also have the same problem. It is easier to raise money for the support of children in institutions where they can be visited and photographed, than for helping them to return home. Sathi is trying to persuade donors to guide their other partners to include budgets for the cost of effecting family reunions in all their programmes, which may be a subtle way of promoting this policy in other agencies.

In the year 2006, when the government introduced the Child Welfare Committees (CWCs), Sathi realized quickly that they are the official lifeline for all children in need of care and protection and are perhaps the only hope nationally for the boys with whom it works. It has been working consistently with the committees to gain entry into some government children's homes, and to conduct camps for their children. Sathi demonstrates its approach to family reunion and its skills in address tracing and counselling to CWCs it is working with. It has been the first NGO to come forward and offer training to CWC members and create learning and networking opportunities for them. Recognizing the need for technical support for CWCs it has located its own counsellors in the Government Homes with the understanding that they will perform a secretarial assistance for CWCs in addition to counselling children.

Sathi's Outreach

In 2013 Sathi was directly working in 11 major railway stations and thirty four GCHs across nine States in India (see Figure A.1). Partner NGOs were also following Sathi's approach in Tirupati, Kolkata and also in Delhi, and others were doing similar work elsewhere. Sathi staff were also seconded to district

Child Welfare Committees. The number of platform locations has varied between 15 and 10 in the last few years depending on availability of resources and the nature of local partnerships. The presence in GCH has been steadily increasing.

Figure A.1:
Sathi Outreach 2012–2013

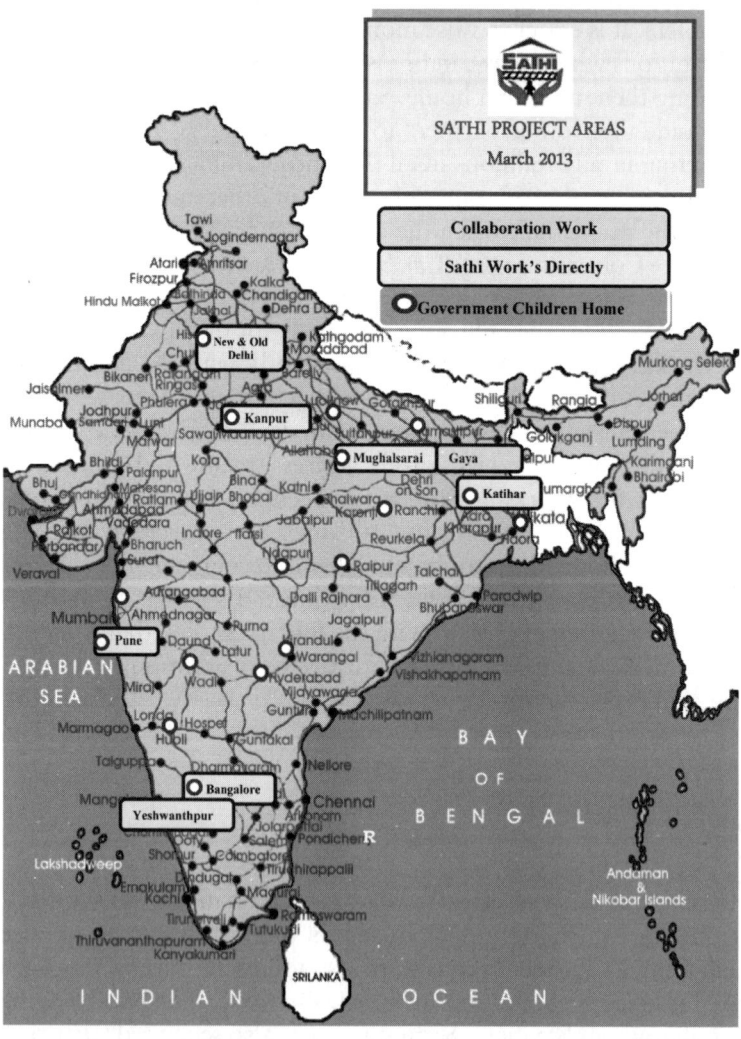

By the end of March 2013, Sathi had reunited nearly 40 thousand runaway children with their parents. The great majority of these children are boys. Sathi does contact some girls, but boys make up 95 per cent or more of the children whom Sathi assists. In the last few years the girls rescued formed roughly 2 per cent of rescues from platforms. There is no reliable data about the number of girls who run away from home, but they are far fewer than boys. This does not mean that there are fewer reasons why young girls should run away from home than boys. The opposite is probably the case, given the sad persistence of prejudice against girls and women at all levels of Indian society.

Sathi managed to gain greater access to children in government homes by 2009. Sathi counsellors worked in these institutions for an initial period of six months and were able to demonstrate techniques of tracing children's addresses to the staff there. Thereafter, the Sathi counsellors worked only with children who have been in the homes for over six months. The numbers are fewer, but the cases more difficult to tackle. The GCH staff have themselves become adept at gathering the needed details from the child and Sathi staff help in address tracing because the staff are usually constrained for access to phones and other modes of communication and travel. In 2013 the CGH staff could reunite 1,250 children with their families taking support from Sathi for address tracing while Sathi team restored 933 children who had been in the GCH for over six months. Sathi has been able to work with many GCHs for girls too. Therefore Sathi staff could reunite 364 girls (39 per cent) and the GCH staff restored 355 girls (28 per cent) with Sathi support for address tracing.

Sathi uses its widespread telephone networks to keep in contact with most of the children they send home. They talk to children's families, and have found that over 90 per cent continue to remain at home. Parents also say that their children's behaviour is better than it was before they ran away. In case of need Sathi is able to provide some financial and other types of assistance to the family.

Figure A.2:
Children Returned Home by Sathi from 2005 to 2013

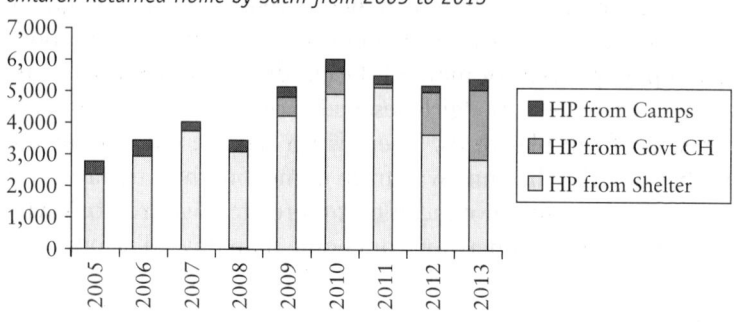

Figure A.3:
Children at Home on Phone Follow-Up

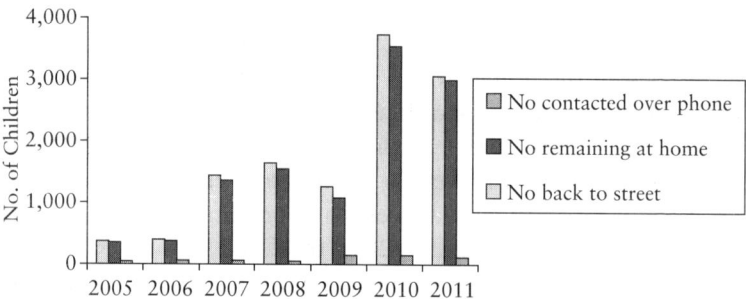

Critiques of the Sathi Approach

Sathi's methods are sometimes contested by others. They argue that if a child resents his family and runs away their decision must be accepted as valid and permanent. Good institutional care can be preferable to a tough family environment which a child has rejected, and if a family fails in its responsibility towards a child it is argued that the state should take over full responsibility for that child. It is therefore wrong to bring subtle or direct pressure on a runaway child to return home. It is surely better, they argue, for a child to be safely accommodated in a good quality institution, where they can develop their own life skills and learn how to achieve emotional social and economic independence. Many NGOs have set up such institutions, and some are indeed of good quality, as also are some of the children's homes which are run by the state. The physical conditions, food, sleeping accommodation, medical care, schooling and in some cases vocational training are of a far higher standard than these children could find from home, and some such institutions are very similar to the private boarding schools, often known as 'public schools', for which middle class families in India, the UK and elsewhere pay very high fees.

There is also a point of view which is against both home and institutions; children who have chosen to live on the street or a railway platform should be allowed to do so, and those who wish to help them should focus their efforts on improving their lives in these places, rather than on taking them away, either to their homes or to institutions. Sathi in fact started in this way. It has been argued that if a runaway returns to an uncaring home, he may have to work, for his family or for others. Sending such children home is tantamount to encouraging child labour, which may be even worse than what they are doing to survive on the platform. It is argued that it is better to ensure that children go back to school and college even if this means that they must live away from their families.

Many others agree in principle that reunion with family is the best option in theory, but they lack the skills or the patience to persist in searching for children's addresses and negotiating with the parents or other family members for the successful return and long-term well-being of the child.

Sathi's performance in the 20 years of its history, clearly shows that home is not only the best place for most runaway children; it is also possible and economic to send them there.

On References and Sources

We were privileged to share a lot of personal information about children, parents and families in the process of collecting material to write this book. We have tried to use all the information and views offered in a manner that does not cross the personal boundaries of confidentiality.

Stories presented in the text boxes are from published sources and we have retained the details as given in the sources. Notes and references are provided at the end of each chapter.

Stories in the narrative part of the text in italics are from either personal interviews or Sathi's documentation and they are presented to explain or illustrate the point being made in the text.

The names of individuals have been changed. Place names have been retained without much masking.

In chapters 3, 4, 5, 6 and 7 we accompany a set of boys and their interface with Sathi beginning on the platform and traversing the shelter, the government home, a Sathi camp and eventually the return to their family and home. These stories are drawn from Sathi's reports and research as well as events we were witness to in our field work. They are not in italics. This device is used to present details of Sathi's methods from the point of view of runaway children and the staff members working with them.

Sathi's website www.sathiindia.org offers various reports and studies for those interested. It also has a link to a blog that describes events in Sathi as they are unfolding.

Index

214 *Rescuing Railway Children*

Don Bosco vocational training institution, 97
driven by children, 137

ECHO, 7
Ehsaas, 128–129
empowerment of street children, 144–145
equality with children, 137
'Every Child Matters', 157

Fakruddin, Baba, 10
for-profit business *vs* not-for-profit organisations, 125–126
foster carers, 160–163

government children's homes, perspectives, 80–84, 101, 184–185
Government Railway Police (GRP), 34, 117, 128, 180

Hart, Roger, 137–139
Hitesh, Jaimala, 10
homecoming
    access to education or vocational training, 104–105
    family financial support, 105
    follow-up of children home-placed through shelter, 112–114
    reunions through shelters, 106–109
    Vishnu's story, 102–103
homes and institutions for children in need, 28–29
Hyderabad Council of Human Welfare, 127

informing children, 137
institutional children's homes, 131
    argument for, 132–135
    experiences in other countries, 150–151
    pros and cons of, 149–150
Integrated Child Protection Scheme (ICPS), 179, 182
Integrated Programme for Street Children (IPSC), 207
international policies and street children, 25

juvenile delinquents, 27
Juvenile Justice Act (JJ Act, 2006), 28, 179
The Juvenile Justice (Care and Protection) Act, 2000, 27
Juvenile Justice (Care & Protection) Amendment Act, 2006, 30, 80
    weaknesses, 35–37
Juvenile Justice system, 28

Kollashany, Father George, 88, 100

looked-after children, 157–160

Mander, Harsh, 35
manipulation of children, 137
MAYA, 99
McDonalds, 125
Minutes of 42nd PAB Meeting, June 2012, 28
Model Rules, 2007, 27

Nair, Mira, 6–7
The National Commission for Protection of Child Rights, (NCPCR), 33–35
    draft guidelines on safety and protection, 34
National Commission for Protection of Child Rights (NCPCR), 180
national policy on children, 27
networking on platforms, 47–48, 125
NGO children's institutions, collaboration efforts, 122, 124–130
    with ActionAid, 127
    in Andhra Pradesh, 126–127
    with Bal Prafulta, 129–130
    with Ehsaas in Lucknow, 128
    with Hyderabad Council of Human Welfare, 127
    with Saathi of Mumbai, 127–128
    with Salam Balak Trust at Delhi, 129
    weaknesses, 130
Norway child care system, 38

Observations cum Special Homes, 28
Oliver Twist, 48

About the Authors

Malcolm Harper is currently an independent consultant. He was educated at Oxford, Harvard and Nairobi Universities. He first worked in marketing in England, and then taught at the University of Nairobi. He was Professor of Enterprise Development at Cranfield School of Management, and since 1995 he has worked independently, mainly in India. His work has in general focused on the application of business management tools to the alleviation of poverty, and he has published extensively on enterprise development, micro-finance and inclusive livelihoods. He was Chairman of Basix Finance in India for 10 years, and is Chairman of M-CRIL, the international microfinance and social rating company. He is chair, trustee and board member of a number of institutions in the United Kingdom, the Netherlands, the United States and India, and has worked on poverty issues in Bangladesh and Pakistan, and in parts of Africa, Latin America etc.

Lalitha Iyer is currently an independent researcher and social consultant. She began her career in the banking sector, joining SBI as an officer in 1976. She left SBI in 1998 to head Vidyaranya, a leading school in Hyderabad. Since 2001 she has been a researcher and consultant in the social development sector. She has been a board member in the Basix Livelihoods group across India, and is now the Chairperson of Sathi.

Kate Bulman is a qualified nurse with a degree in Social Anthropology from the London School Economics of and a Masters Degree from the Institute of Education in London in Health Education. Her focus is on Health Education and she has a particular interest in parenting and families and runs interventions with young men who are fathers or are at risk of becoming fathers at a young age.